DUCHESS AT HOME

DUCHESS *at home*

SWEET & SAVOURY RECIPES FROM MY HOME TO YOURS

by Giselle Courteau

appetite
by RANDOM HOUSE

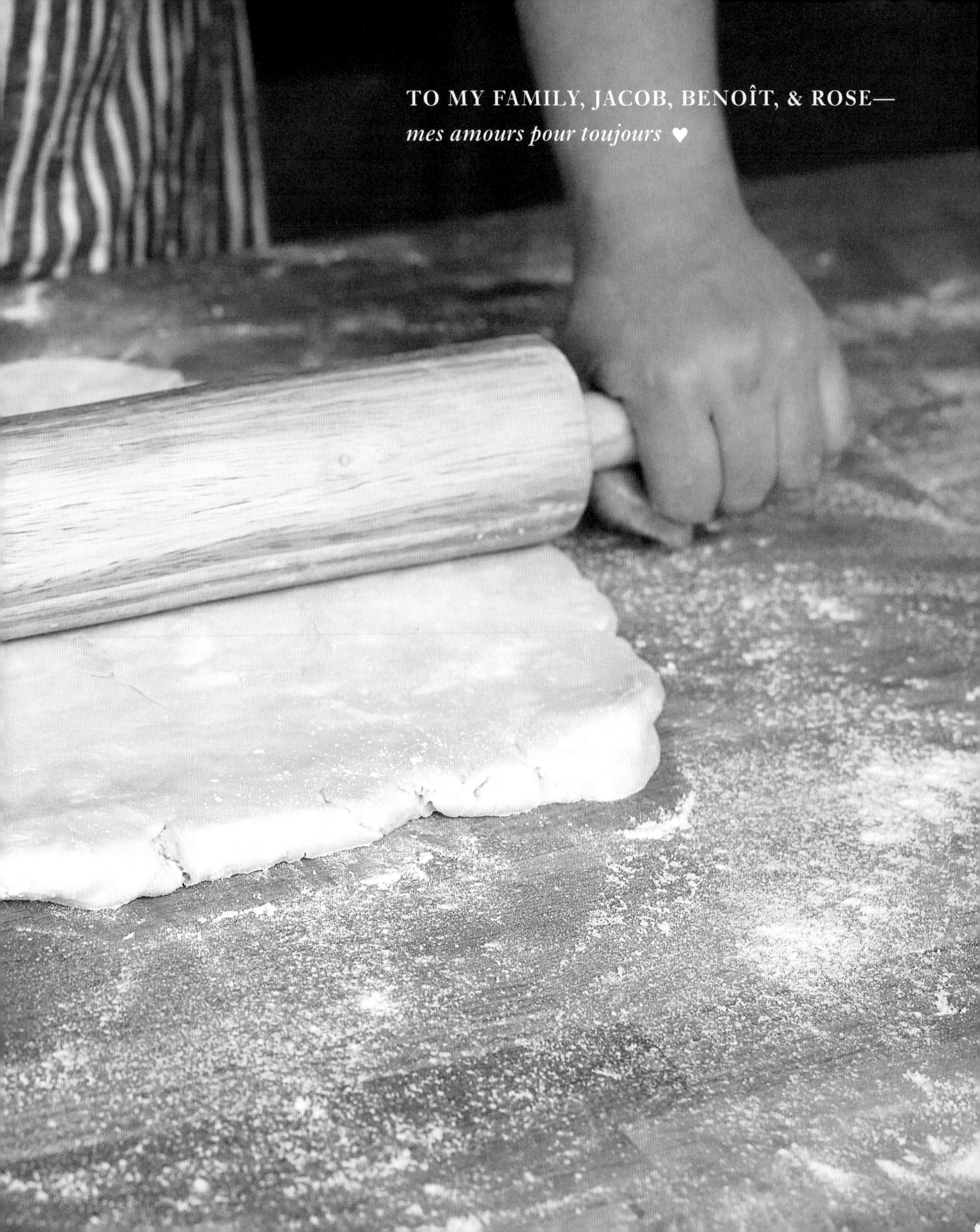

TO MY FAMILY, JACOB, BENOÎT, & ROSE—
mes amours pour toujours ♥

Appetite by Random House® and colophon are registered trademarks of Penguin Random House LLC.

Library and Archives Canada Cataloguing in Publication is available upon request.
ISBN: 978-0-525-61032-8
eBook ISBN: 978-0-525-61033-5

Design and Photography by Sarah Hervieux
Printed and bound in China

Published in Canada by Appetite by Random House®,
a division of Penguin Random House Canada Limited.

www.penguinrandomhouse.ca

10   9   8   7   6   5   4   3   2   1

appetite
by RANDOM HOUSE

Penguin
Random
House

Contents

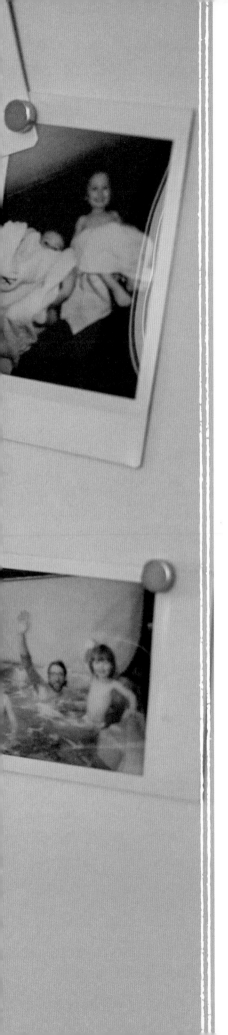

Introduction

IF SOMEBODY HAD TOLD ME 25 YEARS AGO that my life would be what it is now, I wouldn't have believed them. Baking has always been with me, but never would I have imagined that it would become my career and life's work.

As a teenager, I didn't excel at anything specific and my grades at school weren't great, but I did know what made me happy—it was the time I spent at home, baking. I cherished my mother's copy of *Company's Coming Desserts* and looked forward to the holidays when I would be helping her make treats. I thought of becoming a pastry chef, but was encouraged to go to university instead. Yet even after several years of study, I was still really only thinking about pastries—and slowly but surely, my skills and confidence in the kitchen were improving.

At 24, I decided that I was going to open a pastry shop. It took six more years for Duchess Bake Shop to finally come into being and nothing could really have prepared me for what it would be like. Overnight, I went from being a home baker to a small-business owner, with all the stresses and responsibilities that come with it. At first we worked 20-hour days, seven days a week. Doing payroll, paying bills, and bookkeeping were all skills I had to learn on the fly. Those first three years were the most exciting and the most difficult of my life.

With the flurry of the Bake Shop, I completely stopped baking at home. It was when Jacob and I had our children, Benoît and Rose, that I realized how much I missed it. I'm at my happiest when I'm in my home kitchen baking for my family.

It's been five years since *Duchess Bake Shop* was published. In that cookbook I shared the recipes for our most popular pastries at the bakery and tried to bring what we do in a professional kitchen within reach of the home baker. But when I bake at home, the things I tend to make are more often a reflection of me as a person. My French-Canadian heritage, my passion for France, the traditions passed down in my family, and the things I grow in my garden all influence what I like to bake at home.

All of the recipes in this book are truly 'me,' each chapter representing an important part of my life. From old family recipes to new creations, this collection is my heart in a book. I hope these recipes will become your family favourites as well. Bon appétit!

—*Giselle*

How to be

A BETTER HOME BAKER

Whether you are just learning to bake or trying to perfect your craft, baking is a lifelong journey. I still learn something every time I step into the kitchen. I think that the most difficult thing to learn and the biggest area I see people struggle with is when to be precise and when flexibility is needed.

My top tips for every home baker—

PREPARE IN ADVANCE

I'm easily distracted in the kitchen and have had my fair share of disasters over the years. I find that I'm always most successful when I have a plan and I've taken the time to think through what I'm going to make. I always tell my students that before you even start, you can set yourself up for success by doing these simple things—

- Read the recipe from one end to the other. That way you have a clear road map of what's ahead, and you can make a plan in regard to how much time each element will take to make, how much waiting time you need to factor in, and whether some ingredients need to be taken out of the refrigerator in advance so they can be at room temperature when it's time to use them.
- Weigh out all of your ingredients and get your equipment ready. There is nothing worse than scrambling to find an ingredient (or worse, realizing you're out of it!) halfway through your recipe.
- Be realistic and wise with your time. If you need to whip up a dessert at the last minute, don't try to take shortcuts on something that needs to set in the refrigerator for several hours. And if you have lots of time, plan to make certain parts ahead of time so that you can focus on assembly prior to serving.

BE FLEXIBLE WITH BAKING TIMES AND OVEN TEMPERATURES

Everyone's oven is a bit different and will bake things in a different amount of time. I have six identical home ovens in our teaching school, all unpacked brand new on the same day, and two of them run hotter than the other four. We know that and keep an eye on them knowing that things might bake more quickly in them.

Also, the type of bakeware you're using (nonstick or regular) will affect the baking time. Any pan that is dark grey will likely brown your desserts more and bake things a few minutes more quickly. I myself have a variety of both kinds and know to adjust my baking times accordingly.

The moral of the story—when checking for doneness, always use your senses to decide if something's done rather than relying entirely on the timer.

All of the recipes in this book have been tested in a standard oven on the regular bake setting. If you have a convection oven, bake everything at about 25°F (15°C) lower than the recipe says. *Continued* ›

KNOW WHEN IT'S OKAY TO MAKE SUBSTITUTIONS

Part of the fun in baking is learning to express yourself using new flavours or taking a recipe and making it your own. That being said, there is an art to knowing where you can be flexible and where you need to stick to the recipe.

Stick to the recipe when it comes to the core components such as eggs, sugar, flour, and liquid. For example, if you think a recipe has too much sugar and want to cut down on the amount, understand that doing so may affect the structure of the dessert and the way it bakes.

Here's where you can always be flexible—

- **Spices**—Don't like cinnamon? Simply omit it, or replace it with a different spice.
- **Extracts and flavourings**—Same as above.
- **Ingredients to be folded in** just before baking such as chopped nuts, chocolate, coconut, frozen berries...

ALWAYS WEIGH YOUR INGREDIENTS

Use a digital scale—this is vital! See 'Weights & Measurements,' page 22.

USE YOUR HANDS

Baking is a tactile craft. I often see people shy away from getting their hands dirty in the kitchen. Your hands are perfect for tasks like pushing ingredients through a sifter, adding butter chunks to a mixer, or checking if a cake is done. And did you know that washing your hands really well is actually more sanitary than wearing latex gloves? This is because people who wear gloves in the kitchen are likely to not change them when needed and don't wash them as often as they do their hands. This is why you will rarely see a professional wearing gloves in the kitchen.

LEARN TO LOVE PIPING BAGS

Using a piping bag can really help with the assembly and finished look of a dessert. Three piping tips—small round (#803), large round (#809), and large star—will cover most of your pastry needs. My rule of thumb is to always use a piping bag that is way bigger than you think you need (I only use 18-inch bags). Large resealable freezer bags also make good piping bags. I'm not big on reusable piping bags because I can never seem to get them clean and they don't work for piping macarons (which I make often), but feel free to use them if you prefer.

DON'T STRESS ABOUT HOW IT LOOKS

Baking should not be anxiety-inducing or cause your stress levels to go up. The saddest thing for me to hear is that someone didn't serve a dessert they made because it didn't look like the picture. Don't worry if it didn't turn out picture perfect—you baked it from scratch with love, and you took some time for yourself. That in itself is something to be proud of. No one will complain about a tasty yet not-so-perfect-looking dessert!

LEARN FROM YOUR MISTAKES

Mistakes happen, and things may not always turn out the way you planned. Take every misstep as a learning opportunity, make a note of it in your book, and give it another go.

In the kitchen, age 3 and now.

Giselle's Kitchen Confessions—

- I never measure my vanilla or other extracts. I eyeball it every time.
- I always add more spices than a recipe calls for (but tried to keep my love for strong spices under control for this book!).
- I never trust baking times in cookbooks.
- I don't like brightly coloured food and only use food colouring when decorating sugar cookies and making macarons.
- My most used and loved kitchen utensil is the rubber spatula (I own several!). I'm very fussy about which ones I buy. They have to be heat resistant (red handle) and have just the right amount of give. I get very annoyed by a super floppy spatula.
- I have a huge sweet tooth and love most desserts and candy. No discrimination from me!
- I'm a terrible cake and cookie decorator and often rely on Jacob's help to come up with pretty ways to finish desserts.
- In the kitchen at work, one of my biggest pet peeves is when the measuring spoons get pulled apart and I have to hunt down the individual spoons.
- I write notes in all of my cookbooks and dog-ear the corners of pages. This drives Jacob nuts, but for me, a cookbook is meant to be used!
- I'm pretty easygoing in the kitchen and am totally fine with making mistakes or messing up a recipe (it still happens often!). The final look isn't something I concern myself with too much. As long as it tastes good and I had fun making it, that's good enough for me!

MY KITCHEN

The two questions I get asked the most often are what does your kitchen look like, and what kind of oven do you have? I think people imagine that my kitchen is somehow different than everyone else's, when in fact it's pretty ordinary (except my oven!). We live in an old house built in 1950 and had our kitchen redone a few years back *(pictured left)*. It's not huge, but it has lots of cupboard and counter space and extra room to store cookbooks.

It took us a long time to decide on the oven we wanted. After some thought, we chose the AGA Legacy, a British design with two small oven compartments. It took me a few months to get used to baking in it because it runs hot and bakes things really quickly, but now I love it. In our test kitchen at the Bake Shop, we use a more standard Bosch home oven. For this book, after testing the recipes at home I re-tested them in the Bosch oven to ensure that my baking temperatures and times were accurate.

TOOLS & EQUIPMENT

With the absurd amount of kitchen equipment on the market today it's easy to get confused about what bakeware really is essential to own. The cupboards in my own home kitchen used to be bursting at the seams with tools, pans, and single-use gadgets. One day I got so frustrated that I went through everything to root out any item that I almost never used. A few hours later, I had gotten rid of half of the things in my cupboard. I was truly astonished at how many useless things I had bought over the years.

In most cases, there's no need to buy specialized equipment or a lot of brand-new bakeware. I myself have a bit of a ragtag ensemble of bakeware, some nonstick and some really old. I am used to all of my pans and know which ones tend to bake things more quickly and which ones need a bit of extra butter.

By far the most expensive piece of equipment you'll need is a stand mixer. You can get by for some recipes with a hand mixer, but they aren't great for making dough (especially brioche), and often they don't have a 'low' speed setting, which makes it difficult to get nice whipped cream or slowly drizzle in ingredients.

On the next page I provide lists of equipment I consider essential, useful, or nice to have in the kitchen. For notes on jamming and canning equipment, see 'Jars & Sanitizing,' page 245.

ESSENTIAL EQUIPMENT FOR A HOME BAKER

- Digital scale (a must!)
- Stand mixer with paddle, whisk, and dough-hook attachments
- Sifter (I like to use a simple fine-mesh sieve)
- Measuring spoons
- Glass liquid measuring cups: 475 ml (2 cups) and 950 ml (4 cups)
- Plastic bench scraper *(Photo A)*
- 2 large bowls
- 2 medium bowls
- 3 small bowls
- Whisk
- Heatproof spatula
- Pastry brush with natural bristles
- Instant-read digital thermometer
- 2 half sheet pans (or jelly roll pans)
- 2 loaf pans *(Photo D, top right)*
- 2 uncoated 8-inch cake pans (avoid nonstick) *(Photo B, left)*
- Muffin pan
- 9-by-13-inch baking dish *(Photo D, left)*
- 9-inch square baking dish *(Photo D, bottom right)*
- 10-cup bundt pan *(Photo C, top)*
- Wire cooling rack

USEFUL BUT NOT ESSENTIAL

- 18-inch disposable piping bags
- Piping tips: star tip, small round tip (#803), large round tip (#809) *(Photo E)*
- Tart pan with a removable bottom (8-inch round or 14-by-4-inch rectangular) *(Photo F, top)*
- 9- or 10-inch round springform pan *(Photo B, right)*
- Small and large offset spatulas (palette knives)
- Pizza wheel
- Solid round cookie cutter set (various sizes)
- Small ice cream scoop, for cookie dough
- 9- or 10-inch cast-iron pan

NICE TO HAVE

- Shortbread pan *(Photo C, bottom)*
- Madeleine pan *(Photo F, bottom)*
- Clafoutis dish
- 8 individual brioche moulds
- Cake-decorating turntable
- Small electric nut grinder
- Waffle iron
- Ceramic pie weights
- 8 ovenproof ramekins

A note about bakeware coatings—

Nowadays, bakeware comes with a variety of different coatings. For the most part they are fine. The one thing to keep in mind is that if you buy bakeware with a nonstick coating (usually a dark grey colour), then your baked goods will likely bake a bit faster and brown more quickly. Just keep an eye on your baking time. The only bakeware that I own that has to be uncoated is my two 8-inch cake pans. This is because chiffon cake can't be baked in a coated nonstick pan: the chiffon will always collapse because it has nothing to 'stick' to as it crawls up the side of the pan.

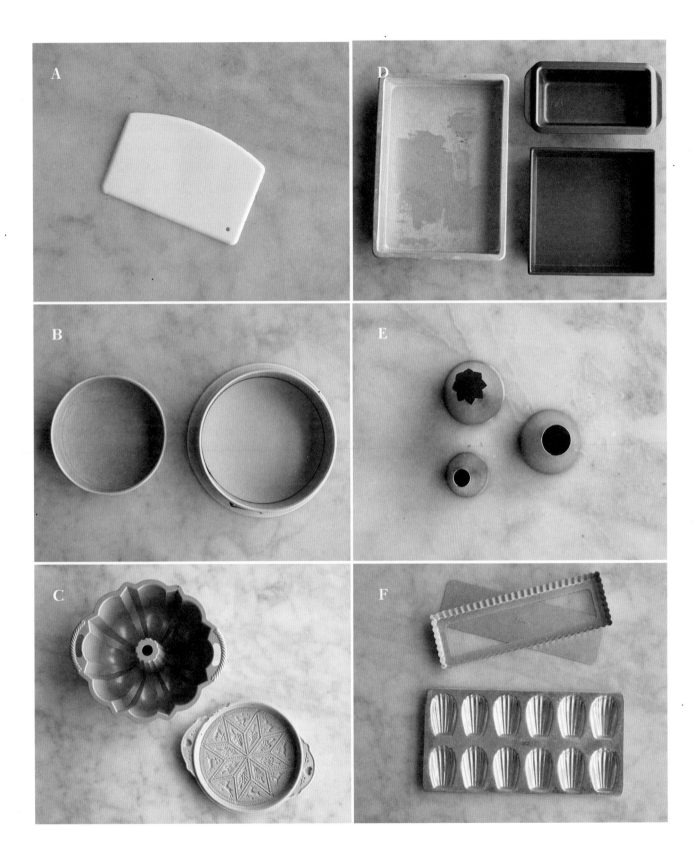

INGREDIENTS
The basics—

I'm big on using the best-quality ingredients I can find. Real vanilla, Valrhona chocolate, and good-quality butter are ingredients I never compromise on. The other important thing for me is to use fresh herbs and fresh citrus, especially when it's a flavour I'm trying to showcase.

BUTTER
Always use unsalted butter in your baking. Because the amount of salt in commercial salted butter varies a lot, it's best that you control the amount of salt in the recipe by adding it in yourself. When a recipe calls for butter to be at room temperature, aim to take it out a couple hours in advance, or even the night before. You can also cube it cold and microwave it at half power to soften it a bit, but make sure it doesn't melt.

CHOCOLATE & COCOA POWDER
In my opinion, the finest baking chocolate is made by Valrhona in France, but there are several other great baking chocolate brands, such as Callebaut and Cocoa Barry. Although buying the best is not easy on the wallet, skimping on quality will really show where chocolate is concerned, especially in a dessert that showcases it. Valrhona makes about 20 varieties of chocolate shaped in their signature 'fèves' (small oval callets), each weighing exactly 3 g. I also use only their alkalized (Dutch-processed) cocoa powder. It's dark and has a high fat content and the deepest chocolate flavour. Just seeing it side by side with most grocery store cocoa will convince you that it's worth the extra money.

EGGS
The standard size of egg we use in baking is 'large,' as marked on egg cartons in the store. The industry standard is that 1 large egg weighs about 55 g (20 g for the yolk and 35 g for the white). The reality, of course, is that no two eggs are the same (hey, chickens, lay your eggs exactly 55 g every time!). In some recipes, I've included a weight for eggs where I consider precision in weight to be important.

FLOUR
The two basic types of flour you should keep in your cupboard for baking are all-purpose flour and cake flour. Stay away from self-rising flours, and keep in mind that substituting whole wheat flour for all-purpose flour can affect your end result. If you will be sifting the flour, always measure it before doing so.

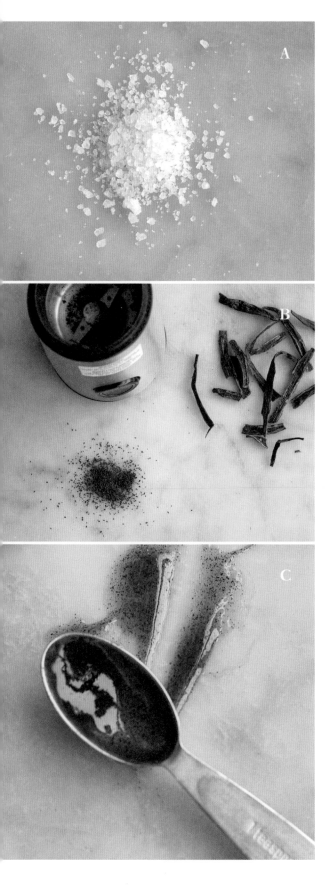

GELATIN

I'm used to using both powdered gelatin and sheet gelatin (the latter more commonly used by professionals). In this book we stick to powdered gelatin because it's what's available in most grocery stores. The main thing to remember when working with gelatin is that the water used to dissolve it needs to be ice cold. A few minutes after mixing the gelatin into the water, it should become firm to the touch. You can then melt it in the microwave and stir it into the base you're trying to set. If 5 minutes after adding the powder to the water it's still soft, it means that it didn't bloom. Throw it out and start again.

SALT *(Photo A)*

Fleur de sel is a delicate, flaky sea salt from France's northern coast. It's a great finishing salt and is used in baking when we want to draw attention to the 'flavour' of salt. Fleur de sel has no iodine in it, making it less harsh on the palate than table salt.

SPICES

I've always assumed that it's standard for everyone to keep a stock of spices in their kitchens. I've only recently realized that for many people that's just not the case. Ground cinnamon, ginger, nutmeg, cloves, and allspice are spices I always have on hand for baking.

VANILLA BEANS *(Photo B)*

With shortages in recent years, we've seen the price of vanilla skyrocket, and the beans are now out of reach for many home bakers. If you do happen to use a vanilla bean, make sure you're getting the most out of it. Once you've scraped all the seeds out, let the vanilla bean dry out on your windowsill for a week. When it's completely dry, use a coffee or spice grinder to grind it into a powder. This can then be used to replace vanilla extract or paste, teaspoon for teaspoon.

VANILLA PASTE *(Photo C)*

Vanilla paste is used in the exact same way, and in the same quantity, as vanilla extract. The biggest difference is that it contains vanilla seeds, which gives it better flavour. Vanilla paste is what I use in all of my baking (including all the desserts at Duchess). It's not cheap, but a little goes a long way.

YEAST

I used to think that using fresh yeast was far superior to using dry. After years of using both, I'm not so convinced that I can really tell the difference. If you have easy access to fresh yeast, by all means use it, but dry yeast tends to be much easier for home bakers to get their hands on and, in my opinion, will perform just as well. See 'Yeast Facts' (page 39) for more information about yeast.

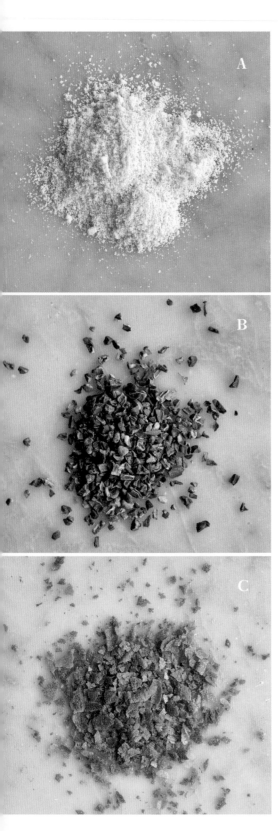

INGREDIENTS
Handy to have around—

There is a handful of useful ingredients that I recommend you have on hand. It's pretty easy to purchase the majority of them in specialty stores or online. You may not use these items very often, but they don't go bad and can sit in your cupboard indefinitely.

ALCOHOL
I always have a bottle each of brandy, cognac, dark rum, and kirsch (cherry liqueur) on hand.

ALMOND FLOUR *(finely ground almonds) (Photo A)*
Almond flour is the foundation of so many traditional French pastries. Buying the finest and freshest grind you can is very important. If you will only be using it sporadically, store it in the freezer in a well-sealed container or a resealable freezer bag.

BUTTERMILK POWDER
A revelation to many, buttermilk powder is possibly the most useful thing I have in my cupboard. Although nothing can quite replace fresh buttermilk, freeze-dried buttermilk reconstituted with water is much better than the makeshift option of adding vinegar to milk. This is by far the most popular ingredient we sell in our baking school.

COCOA NIBS *(Photo B)*
Cocoa nibs are cocoa beans crushed up into little tiny pieces. They aren't sweet and add a nice crunch to cookies or make a pretty garnish to finish desserts.

EGG ALBUMEN
Also known as egg-white powder, this is the key ingredient in French macarons. It also works wonders in royal icing for decorating sugar cookies.

FEUILLETINE *(Photo C)*
This crunchy praline cereal adds great texture to melted chocolate. Although you can use cornflakes cereal as a substitute, the wafer-thin texture and crunch of feuilletine is hard to beat.

FRUIT POWDER *(Photo D)*

Freeze-dried fruit ground to a powder is a great way to add flavour to baking, especially in whipped ganache. It's all-natural, and a little goes a long way. I usually keep raspberry and strawberry on hand.

PEARL SUGAR *(Photo E)*

Popular in Europe, pearl sugar, sometimes referred to as nib sugar, is a hard sugar that doesn't melt well at standard oven temperatures. It's most often used to decorate brioches, cream puffs, and sweet breads, and it's also a key component in the traditional Liège waffle.

RICE FLOUR

Sometimes called for in recipes to enhance texture, rice flour is easy to purchase in any Asian supermarket.

TONKA BEANS *(Photo F)*

These beans have a scent and flavour that is a bit difficult to pin down—some say it reminds them of vanilla; others detect cherries, cinnamon, or pepper, with a subtle smokiness. Although a bit tricky to find in stores, in Canada they are readily available online. For a sensational flavour twist, in any recipe that calls for vanilla bean seeds, you can replace them with finely grated tonka bean.

An Important Note on
WEIGHTS & MEASUREMENTS

MOST OF US GREW UP USING CUPS TO MEASURE OUR RECIPES, and a lot of our family recipes or reliable standbys list only those. They almost always turn out fine because we've been doing it for so long and we know our recipes that work. Though I have a healthy respect for my grandmother's recipes in cups (which I still make in cups), it took me years to understand that the whole system of measuring using cups is actually quite flawed.

Transitioning from being a home baker to working in a kitchen with professionals was quite a steep learning curve for me. The very first lesson I learned—and the most important one—is that no professional in the culinary world would ever dream of measuring by volume—that is, using measuring cups. The reason? Because more often than not it is inaccurate, and the goal is to be as precise and consistent as possible. That means measuring by weight using a digital kitchen scale. Using cups can cause many frustrations for not only the baker but also the person who wrote the recipe.

If you look on the internet for a conversion of cups to grams, you won't be able to find a consistent answer. The main reasons for this are that everyone has their own measuring technique, and ingredients can come packaged differently or packed down to varying degrees. Take almond flour, for example: it can be really compressed or light as air, which means that its weight can swing wildly from 50 to 250 g per cup. Even an ingredient like sugar isn't always consistent. Universally on the internet, 1 cup of sugar weighs 200 g, but for me personally, it's almost always 230 g. That's a pretty big difference!

The following ingredients are notoriously difficult to measure accurately with cups—

- All-purpose flour
- Cake flour
- Icing sugar
- Brown sugar (is it lightly packed, firmly packed… and what do those even mean?)
- Almond flour
- Cocoa powder
- Chocolate (are they chunks, chips, large pieces?)
- Butter (it's the worst to try to scrape it out of a cup!)

To check the human element in how ingredients get measured, I conducted a test…

I asked 10 random people to each measure 1 cup of flour (from the same source) five times, and each time I weighed their results. I found a huge fluctuation from one person to the next, with the weights ranging from 125 to 180 g per cup—but each person was quite consistent in their own weights. My own weights were on the high side at 160 g per cup.

This was startling, especially considering that flour is such a basic ingredient in baking. I noticed that each person had their own way of measuring: the light scoop and scrape, the scoop and shake, the scoop and bang on the counter… I even had someone sift the flour before measuring it (never do this, by the way, unless a recipe specifically asks you to!). It was obvious that people's unique way of measuring dramatically affected how much flour got measured.

For this book, I decided to use the average from my test as my guideline for all-purpose flour, which was 145 g per cup. My rule of thumb now is that if a recipe has a weight listed, I always use that instead of the cups, even for wet ingredients. Using a digital kitchen scale is really the most accurate way to bake and can make you a better baker.

HOW TO CHOOSE A KITCHEN SCALE
Digital kitchen scales are easily found in any kitchen store or online. A decent one will cost about $40, and there is no need to buy one with too many features. Look for these two main things—

1 Make sure the scale is accurate to 1 g. Some scales are only accurate to 5 g. For finicky recipes, you'll want it to be more accurate than that.

2 Check that it doesn't have a feature that automatically turns it off after a short period of time. I once had a scale that would turn itself off after 1 minute of non-use. Often it would take me more time than that to get my next ingredient, and I would constantly have to be starting over. *Continued ›*

HOW TO USE A KITCHEN SCALE

There are a couple of ways that you can use your digital scale to weigh ingredients. My sister likes to weigh her ingredients one at a time and then transfer them to a separate bowl. I like to weigh out the ingredients that belong together in a single bowl, zeroing the scale between each ingredient. I weigh things out in different corners of the bowl. That way, if I weigh too much, I can easily scoop some out while leaving the other ingredients untouched.

Here's an example of how I use my digital scale, weighing out 50 g each of flour and sugar.

1   Turn on the scale.

2   Place a bowl on the scale and press the 'zero' button (labelled 'tare' on some scales) to set the weight to 0 *(Photo A)*.

3   Weigh out 50 g flour *(Photo B)*.

4   Press 'zero' to reset the scale to 0 *(Photo C)*.

5   Weigh out 50 g sugar *(Photo D)* and press 'zero.'

Continue this process until you've weighed all of your dry ingredients together in the same bowl. In a new bowl, use the same method to weigh out your wet ingredients.

Déjeuner en famille
FAMILY BREAKFAST

BREAKFAST, MY FAVOURITE MEAL OF THE DAY, is something we take pretty seriously in our family. It's important for me to have a few easy recipes that I can whip up in a pinch, as well as a few more intricate ones that are suitable for having family and friends over for brunch. Although my busy schedule sometimes has me eating a quick breakfast on the go, I still like to make an effort a few times a week to have a special breakfast at home. In this chapter you will find some simple make-ahead options as well as some dazzlers to wow your guests.

"WHAT NICER THING CAN YOU DO FOR SOMEBODY
THAN MAKE THEM BREAKFAST?"
—ANTHONY BOURDAIN

PANCAKES *with* *Spiced Maple Strawberries*

SPICED MAPLE STRAWBERRIES

300 g (2–3 cups) fresh strawberries, hulled, quartered (if large)
2 Tbsp maple syrup
1 Tbsp maple or granulated sugar
pinch of ground cinnamon
pinch of ground cloves
pinch of ground allspice
pinch of freshly ground black pepper

PANCAKES

220 g (1½ cups) all-purpose flour
2 Tbsp sugar
2 tsp baking powder
1 tsp baking soda
¼ tsp salt
⅛ tsp ground nutmeg
350 g (1½ cups) buttermilk
2 large eggs
35 g (3 Tbsp) vegetable oil
1 tsp vanilla extract or paste
maple syrup, to serve

INGREDIENT NOTES

If you buy strawberries in the dead of winter (what I call cardboard strawberries), make sure you choose ripe and undamaged ones and cut off any white parts.

For the buttermilk, you can use reconstituted buttermilk powder if you don't have fresh—but did you know that you can freeze fresh buttermilk? That means you can buy it without fear of wasting what you don't immediately use. I like to freeze mine in 1½-cup portions in resealable plastic bags, easy to pull out as needed. Transfer it to the refrigerator the night before making the pancakes, or if you're in a hurry, run the frozen bag under a tap of hot water to thaw quickly.

EQUIPMENT

You will need a nonstick frying pan or a griddle.

The best pancakes I've ever had were topped with strawberries sweet like candy and drizzled with maple syrup. The secret? The fruit had been macerated. This process—adding sugar to fruit to enhance the flavour and draw out liquid—is very simple. Make sure you use good-quality, ripe, fresh fruit to get the most out of the maceration.

TO MAKE THE SPICED MAPLE STRAWBERRIES

1 In a bowl, mash about ¼ cup of the strawberries with a fork. Add the remaining ingredients and gently mix until well combined.

2 Cover and set aside at room temperature for at least 30 minutes, or in the refrigerator for at least 1 hour.

TO MAKE THE PANCAKES

3 Combine all the dry ingredients in a bowl. Whisk well, making sure there are no lumps. In another bowl, whisk together the remaining ingredients.

4 Add the wet ingredients to the dry and whisk until the larger lumps have disappeared.

5 Heat a nonstick pan over medium heat or plug in your griddle. I like to use a bit of butter in my nonstick pan but don't feel it's necessary on my griddle. Once hot, pour quarter-cup circles of pancake batter and cook until small bubbles are popping on the surface. Flip and cook until brown. Try to disturb them as little as possible as they cook.

6 Serve hot out of the pan, topped with the macerated strawberries and a generous drizzle of maple syrup.

STORAGE

Try to avoid leaving the strawberries in the refrigerator for more than a day, as they will become soggy. Both the pancakes and the macerated strawberries can be frozen for up to three months.

KUGELHOPF

Serves 12—

RAISINS
120 g (¾ cup) raisins
2 Tbsp kirsch liqueur
2 Tbsp water

PRE-FERMENT
165 g (⅔ cup) whole milk
75 g (½ cup) all-purpose flour
10 g (3 tsp) active dry yeast

15 whole peeled almonds

DOUGH
290 g (2 cups) all-purpose flour
50 g (⅓ cup) icing sugar
2 tsp salt
2 large eggs
2 tsp orange-blossom water
zest of 1 orange
135 g (½ cup + 2 Tbsp) unsalted butter,
    cubed, at room temperature
additional butter, softened, for the
    kugelhopf mould
additional icing sugar, for dusting the
    kugelhopf

SIMPLE SYRUP *(optional)*
50 g (¼ cup) sugar
60 g (¼ cup) water
¼ tsp orange-blossom water

EQUIPMENT
You will need a stand mixer fitted with a
dough-hook attachment and a kugelhopf
mould or a 10-cup bundt pan.

This sweet breakfast bread from the Alsace region of France is one of my all-time favourite foods. I love a thick slice, still warm out of the oven, with my favourite jam or a big smear of butter. Similar to Italian panettone, kugelhopf is made with the distinct Alsatian flavours of kirsch and orange and is gently sweet and soft in texture.

Christine Ferber, a pastry chef and jam-maker extraordinaire I greatly admire, makes an incredibly flavourful and delicious classic version of this bread. Her advice is to bake it in a traditional earthenware mould that you never wash. The idea is that each family's mould develops its own 'seasoning' over time for its own unique flavour. The earthenware mould I bought in her shop in Alsace years ago is one of my most treasured possessions. I gently wipe it after each use and proudly display it in my kitchen.

PROCEDURE

1   Place the raisins in a small bowl or container with the kirsch and water. Cover and set aside overnight. The raisins should plump up and absorb most of the liquid.

2   To make the pre-ferment, warm the milk to 26–32°C to activate the yeast *(see 'Yeast Facts,' page 39)*. Place it in a stand mixer bowl and mix in the flour and yeast. Cover with a cloth or plastic wrap and set aside for about 20 minutes.

3   While the pre-ferment is sitting, place the almonds in a small bowl and cover with boiling water. Set aside to soak.

4   Once the pre-ferment is ready, fit the bowl on a stand mixer fitted with a dough-hook attachment. Add the flour, icing sugar, salt, eggs, orange-blossom water, and orange zest and mix on low speed until all the ingredients are well incorporated. *Continued ›*

5   Still on low speed, gradually add the butter, a few cubes at a time. Once all the butter has been added *(Photo A)*, turn the mixer up to medium and continue mixing until the dough is smooth, shiny, elastic, and soft and has pulled away from the sides of the bowl. This should take 5 to 10 minutes.

6   Drain off any excess liquid from the raisins. Remove the bowl from the stand mixer and fold the raisins into the dough by hand.

7   Cover and set aside to proof in a warm area for 1 to 1½ hours, until doubled in size.

8   While the dough is proofing, prepare your kugelhopf mould. Brush the mould generously with softened butter, making sure to get it in all the grooves. Drain the almonds, dry them off with a paper towel, and place one in the bottom of each groove *(Photo B)*.

9   Once proofed *(Photo B)*, transfer the dough to a clean surface and knead briefly to remove any air bubbles. Using the end of a rolling pin, make a hole in the centre of the dough. Place the dough ring into the mould, gently pressing it down into all the grooves *(Photo C)*.

10 Fill a shallow pan or 9-by-13-inch baking dish with the hottest water you can get out of your tap (not boiling) and place it on the bottom surface of your oven. Place the kugelhopf on an oven rack and close the oven door.

11 Let the kugelhopf proof in the oven for 1½ to 2 hours, until doubled in size. Try not to open the oven door for the first 45 minutes as you want the steam to create a humid environment inside the oven. *Continued ›*

12 Once proofed *(Photo D)*, remove the pan of water and the kugelhopf from the oven. Arrange your oven racks so that the kugelhopf will sit in the centre of the oven with no rack above it (as it may puff up). Preheat your oven to 390°F (200°C), then put in the kugelhopf and immediately reduce the temperature to 350°F (180°C). Bake for 45 to 55 minutes (35 to 40 minutes if using a bundt pan), until the top is a dark golden brown *(Photo E)*.

13 Let the kugelhopf rest for 15 minutes and unmould onto a cooling rack. If any of the almonds have detached, place them back in the grooves on top of the kugelhopf. Dust the top with icing sugar.

Note: To add a bit more sweetness to your kugelhopf, you can brush it with simple syrup prior to dusting it with icing sugar *(optional)*. While the kugelhopf is baking, make the syrup by placing the sugar and water in a small saucepan. Bring to a boil to dissolve the sugar. Remove from heat and add the orange-blossom water. Brush the still-warm kugelhopf with the syrup as soon as it is unmoulded.

SERVING & STORAGE

Kugelhopf is best eaten the day it's baked. It will keep for up to four days and makes excellent toast after the first day.

Café Linnea
BREAKFAST BOWL

OVERNIGHT OATS

150 g (1½ cups) old-fashioned rolled oats

360 g (1½ cups) vanilla almond milk

2 Tbsp almond butter or natural peanut butter, melted

2 Tbsp maple syrup

a few drops vanilla extract

GRANOLA

140 g (1¼ cups) old-fashioned rolled oats

50 g (½ cup) ribbon or shredded unsweetened coconut

85 g (¾ cup) almonds, sliced or roughly chopped

80 g (¾ cup) almond flour

125 g (⅔ cup) dried currants, raisins, or dried apricots, roughly chopped

60 g (½ cup) walnuts or pecans, roughly chopped

75 g (½ cup) pumpkin seeds

35 g (¼ cup) sunflower seeds

3 Tbsp chia seeds

½ tsp ground cinnamon

pinch of salt

3 Tbsp maple syrup or melted honey

3 Tbsp vegetable oil or melted coconut oil

½ tsp vanilla extract or paste

TOPPINGS

about 1 cup vanilla or plain yogurt

about 1 cup fruit compote or ¼ cup jam

almond or peanut butter, melted

fresh fruit *(optional)*

EQUIPMENT

You will need a baking sheet.

With two small children and early mornings, I'm always a bit hard-pressed to make myself breakfast. On really busy days, I get our sister restaurant, Café Linnea, to make me one of their delicious breakfast bowls to give me plenty of energy to get through a busy morning at Duchess. They make everything from scratch, including their almond milk, crème fraîche, and fruit compote, so making it myself before coming to Duchess always seemed out of reach.

With a few tips from Kelsey, the chef at Café Linnea, we devised a faster way to make this at home. A simple step the night before and one batch of granola that lasts the whole week means I can throw it together quickly in the morning now. For something a little less sweet, use unsweetened plain yogurt and top it off with fresh fruit instead of jam or compote.

TO MAKE THE OVERNIGHT OATS

1   In a bowl, mix all of the ingredients together. Cover and leave to soak overnight in the refrigerator.

TO MAKE THE GRANOLA

2   Spray the baking sheet with vegetable oil. Preheat your oven to 275°F (135°C).

3   In a bowl, mix together all the dry ingredients.

4   In a small bowl, combine the maple syrup with the oil and vanilla. Drizzle about three-quarters of it over the dry mixture. Stir to coat evenly.

5   Spread the granola evenly on the baking sheet and bake for 20 minutes. Stir the granola around and drizzle with the remainder of the maple syrup mixture. Bake for an additional 20 minutes, or until lightly browned and toasted. Set aside to cool.
Continued ›

INGREDIENT NOTE

Don't be deterred by the granola's long list of ingredients. Visiting the bulk section of your grocery store is a great way to buy exactly what you need. My family loves this granola so much that I will often double the recipe, spreading the granola out over two baking sheets. You can substitute any of the nuts or dried fruit to suit your taste.

TO ASSEMBLE THE BREAKFAST BOWLS

6   Divide the overnight oats into 4 bowls (or fewer portions if desired). Top each portion with a couple spoonfuls each of yogurt, compote, and granola, and a drizzle of melted almond butter. Top with fresh fruit if desired.

SERVING & STORAGE

These breakfast bowls should be eaten as soon as they are assembled. The oats will keep for up to three days in the refrigerator, so you can put together a bowl just for yourself every morning until they run out. You will have extra granola that can be stored at room temperature in an airtight jar or container for up to six months.

INGREDIENTS

240 g (1 cup) 2% or 1% milk

40 g fresh yeast, or 14 g (4 tsp) active dry
yeast

470 g (3¼ cups) all-purpose flour

40 g (⅓ cup) cocoa powder

25 g (3 Tbsp) icing sugar

½ tsp salt

25 g (1 Tbsp) liquid honey

1 large egg

225 g (1 cup) unsalted butter, cubed,
at room temperature

150 g (1 cup) pearl sugar

fresh fruit, whipped cream, and icing
sugar, for garnish

INGREDIENT NOTE

Popular in Europe, pearl sugar, or nib sugar,
is a hard sugar that doesn't melt at standard
oven temperatures. It's most often used to
decorate brioches, cream puffs, and sweet
breads, and it's also a key component in the
traditional Liège waffle. Pearl sugar can be
tricky to find in stores in North America but
is easily found online.

EQUIPMENT

You will need a waffle iron and a stand mixer
fitted with a dough-hook attachment.

Waffle irons vary greatly in quality and
functionality. Mine is nothing fancy but does
the trick. Make sure your waffle iron is on a
medium-high setting and really hot before
putting in your batter. The pearl sugar will
caramelize and leave behind a bit of a sticky
mess. To clean the waffle iron, let it cool and
gently use a wooden utensil to scrape off the
sugar. Because most waffle irons are nonstick,
it should come off pretty easily.

Chocolate
LIÈGE WAFFLES

*Liège is a city in Belgium known for these famous little
waffles, the delight of locals and visitors alike since the
eighteenth century. Because they are made with a yeasted
dough, their texture is denser, heavier, and more bread-like
than traditional North American–style waffles. Although
I can happily eat these for breakfast, they may verge more
on the brunch or afternoon snack side of things because
of the inclusion of pearl sugar. The sugar adds a crunchy
caramelization bordering on dessert that will have you
addicted from the first bite.*

*In researching the Liège waffle, I found so many
versions that claimed to be 'the original' that I became a
bit overwhelmed. I decided to use my instincts and come up
with a recipe that most resembled the taste and texture that
I remember from my many trips to Europe. Selfishly, I've
also added one of my favourite elements—chocolate—but
you can replace the cocoa powder with additional regular
all-purpose flour if you want to enjoy a more traditional
version of this waffle.*

PROCEDURE

1   In a small bowl, warm the milk slightly so that it will
activate the yeast (but not too hot or it will kill it)
(see 'Yeast Facts,' page 39). Stir in the yeast until
dissolved. Set aside for 10 minutes.

2   Meanwhile, in a stand mixer bowl, combine the
flour, cocoa powder, icing sugar, and salt by hand.
Make a well in the centre and add the honey, egg,
and dissolved yeast and milk.

3   Fit the bowl on the stand mixer fitted with a dough-
hook attachment and mix on low speed until the
ingredients start to come together. Still on low,
gradually add the butter, a few cubes at a time.
Continued ›

4 Once all the butter has been added, turn the mixer up to medium and continue to mix until the dough is smooth and shiny and has pulled away from the sides of the bowl. This should take 5 to 10 minutes.

5 Shape the dough into a ball and place it seam side down in the stand mixer bowl. Cover and let rise at room temperature for 30 minutes *(Photo A)*.

6 Punch the dough down and, using your hands, fold in the pearl sugar. Divide the dough into 12 balls of about 100 g each *(Photo B)*. Cover and chill for at least 45 minutes, until cold and firm. Alternatively, you can refrigerate the dough overnight, work the pearl sugar into it, divide it, and proceed to step 7.

7 To bake, heat your waffle iron to medium-high. Place a ball of dough in the centre of each compartment *(Photo C)*, firmly press down, and close the iron. Bake the waffles until a dark golden brown. The amount of time it takes to bake the waffles perfectly depends on your waffle iron: if you have a traditional European one, it may only take 4 minutes, while most North American ones will require 5 to 7 minutes.

8 Remove the waffles with a fork, being very careful not to touch the caramelized sugar to avoid burning yourself. Garnish with fresh fruit, whipped cream, and icing sugar.

SERVING & STORAGE

Liège waffles are best eaten fresh out of the waffle iron. The baked waffles can be frozen for up to three months and reheated in a toaster or microwave.

YEAST FACTS

Active Dry Yeast

Fresh Yeast

There's an ongoing debate among bread bakers over whether using fresh yeast is better than dry. Those who advocate for using fresh yeast claim that it has a milder and sweeter taste, giving the bread a better overall flavour. They also feel it performs better by activating quickly and staying active longer.

However, many master bakers claim that these differences are so minor they're nearly impossible to perceive, especially when it comes to taste. I used to think that using fresh yeast would provide me with a better bread, but after doing extensive testing I have not been able to tell much of a difference. If you can get your hands on fresh yeast, great, but if you use dry, you will likely get a result that's just as good.

IMPORTANT YEAST TEMPERATURES

- Activated between 26°C (79°F) and 32°C (90°F)
- Damaged at 46°C (115°F) and killed at 63°C (145°F)
- Slowed at 19°C (66°F) and no activity 4°C (39°F)

ACTIVE DRY YEAST

- It has a very long shelf life and is good for up to six months (or until the expiry date on the jar) in your cupboard or refrigerator, as long as it's well sealed.
- It is easy to use—generally you will simply be asked to mix it with warm water and wait for it to activate.
- Avoid using the instant version as the strength can be variable, which makes it a bit unpredictable.

FRESH YEAST *(cake yeast / compressed yeast)*

- It will keep for two weeks well-wrapped in the refrigerator. After that it starts to lose its strength and can go bad.
- It can be frozen, but it will lose 5–10% of its strength. It must be thawed slowly and used within 24 hours of being thawed.
- It should break with a clean edge, crumble easily, and have the texture of soft clay.
- The smell should not be unpleasant and should remind you almost of a sweet yeasted apple.

CONVERTING ACTIVE DRY TO FRESH YEAST

- Use half the amount of dry yeast that has been called for fresh. For example, if a recipe calls for 16 g fresh yeast, use 8 g active dry yeast.

White Wine
PAIN PERDU

Serves 8—

INGREDIENTS

200 g (1 cup) sugar

½ tsp ground cinnamon

¼ tsp ground ginger

¼ tsp ground nutmeg

3 large eggs

zest of one orange

240 g (1 cup) white wine

75 g (⅓ cup) unsalted butter, melted and cooled

5 cups (about half a loaf) stale French bread, cut into 1- to 2-inch cubes

50 g (½ cup) sliced almonds

50 g (⅓ cup) dried currants, raisins, or cranberries

35 g (¼ cup) crystallized ginger

INGREDIENT NOTE

For the wine, I like to use a sauvignon blanc for its acidity, but feel free to use any left-over white wine you might have. For a nicer flavour, steer clear of 'cooking wine' and stick with something that you would normally drink.

EQUIPMENT

You will need a 9-inch baking dish.

Pain perdu, literally 'lost bread,' usually refers to French toast, bread pudding, or any dish where stale bread is used to soak up liquid and cooked, thus giving it new life (the bread is no longer lost!).

In this recipe, the combination of almonds, citrus, and white wine really elevates it and makes it more sophisticated than your standard bread pudding. Don't worry—the alcohol evaporates during baking, which makes this a suitable dish for adults and children alike.

PROCEDURE

1   Preheat your oven to 350°F (180°C). Butter the baking dish.

2   In a large bowl, whisk together the sugar, cinnamon, ginger, nutmeg, eggs, and orange zest.

3   Add the wine and slowly whisk in the butter until well combined.

4   Add the bread cubes, sliced almonds, currants, and crystallized ginger and, using your hands, toss to make sure that all the pieces of bread are well coated. Let soak for 10 minutes.

5   Pour the mixture into the baking dish and bake for 45 to 50 minutes, until the top is golden brown and crispy.

SERVING & STORAGE

This bread pudding is best eaten the day it's made. It will keep at room temperature for up to three days and should be reheated prior to serving.

All-Day Breakfast
MUFFINS

INGREDIENTS

145 g (1 cup) all-purpose flour
1½ tsp baking powder
½ tsp salt
¼ tsp ground black pepper
4 large eggs
2 large egg whites
230 g (1 cup) cottage cheese
150 g (1 cup) cheese curds, roughly
   chopped
75 g (½ cup) diced ham
1 Tbsp finely chopped fresh chives
2 tsp finely chopped fresh rosemary
2 tsp finely chopped fresh thyme

INGREDIENT NOTE

If you can't find cheese curds, these muffins
also work nicely using only cottage cheese—
just increase it to 460 g (2 cups). You may
need to add an extra ½ tsp salt if the ham you
are using isn't very salty. For a vegetarian
option, omit the ham and add ½ tsp salt.

EQUIPMENT

You will need a 12-cavity muffin pan.

These savoury muffins are absolutely craveable! I've fused
a traditional Jewish cottage-cheese muffin with a soufflé,
and for a French-Canadian twist, I've added squeaky cheese
curds. There's a satisfaction in pulling a warm muffin
apart and stretching the curd into the perfect string.

These muffins whip up in no time. Make them ahead to
enjoy throughout the week, or serve a fresh batch to your
brunch guests. With this flexible recipe you can use any
combination of herbs or cured meats that strikes your fancy.

PROCEDURE

1 Spray the muffin pan with vegetable oil. Preheat
   your oven to 400°F (200°C).

2 In a large bowl whisk together the flour, baking
   powder, salt, and pepper.

3 In a separate bowl, whisk together the eggs and
   egg whites until well combined. Fold in the cottage
   cheese, cheese curds, ham, and herbs.

4 Using a spatula, gently mix the wet ingredients into
   the dry.

5 Using an ice cream scoop or a spoon, divide the
   batter evenly among the muffin cups.

6 Bake for 25 to 30 minutes, until a light golden
   brown and the tops spring back to the touch.

SERVING & STORAGE

These muffins are best eaten warm out of the oven.
They will keep for up to five days in the refrigerator
and are great reheated in the oven or the microwave.

MUFFINS

Makes 12 large muffins—

CRUMB TOPPING
45 g (½ cup) old-fashioned rolled oats
50 g (⅓ cup) all-purpose flour
50 g (¼ cup firmly packed) brown sugar
¼ tsp ground cinnamon
60 g (¼ cup) unsalted butter, at room
   temperature

MUFFINS
290 g (2 cups) all-purpose flour
90 g (1 cup) old-fashioned rolled oats
   (not instant)
130 g (⅔ cup firmly packed) golden brown
   sugar
1¾ tsp baking powder
½ tsp baking soda
½ tsp ground cinnamon
½ tsp salt
240 g (1 cup) whole milk
115 g (½ cup) vegetable oil
2 large eggs
1 banana, mashed
1 tsp vanilla extract or paste
250 g (2 cups) mixed fresh or frozen
   berries *(see note)*

INGREDIENT NOTE
I always find it easier to use frozen berries
when baking. Fresh ones are so delicate and
can end up making quite a mess of your batter.
If I only have fresh berries on hand, I pop
them in the freezer while I make my batter
to get them to firm up a bit. If you use fresh
berries, mix the batter as delicately as possible so as to not crush them.

EQUIPMENT
You will need a 12-cavity muffin pan.

*My best friend used to make these for me for break-
fast when I visited her in the mountains. We call them
'Mountain Muffins' because they are perfect for eating
warm out of the oven before hitting the slopes on a cold
winter's day or heading out for a hike. You can use any
berries you like—my favourite combination is raspberries,
blueberries, and blackberries.*

TO MAKE THE CRUMB TOPPING
1 In a bowl, combine the oats, flour, brown sugar, and
   cinnamon. Add the butter and, using your hands,
   work it into the dry ingredients until large clumps
   form. Set aside.

TO MAKE THE MUFFINS
2 Preheat your oven to 375°F (190°C). Spray the
   muffin pan with vegetable oil.

3 In a large bowl, mix together all the dry ingredients.
   If necessary, use your hands to break up any large
   brown-sugar clumps.

4 In a separate bowl, whisk together all the wet
   ingredients.

5 Using a spatula, gently mix the wet ingredients, except
   the berries, into the dry. Add the berries and stir until
   just combined.

6 Using an ice cream scoop or a spoon, divide the
   batter evenly among the 12 muffin cups. The batter
   will fill the muffin cups almost to the top. Distribute
   the crumb evenly over the tops of the muffins.

7 Bake for 25 to 30 minutes, until a toothpick inserted
   in the centre of a muffin comes out clean.

STORAGE
These muffins will keep at room temperature for up to
three days.

PÂTES à TARTINER

Little jars of spreads, compotes, and jams can always be found in abundance in my refrigerator at home. Although making your own pâtes à tartiner—spreads —may seem intimidating, it's actually incredibly easy to do. Having a few different kinds on hand can easily make for a quick breakfast on toast or an afternoon snack—or can help spruce up a brunch.

    Here are three of my favourite pâtes à tartiner to have ready to go. All three lean to the sweet side, but who doesn't love to indulge in a little chocolate at breakfast? The praline version is a bit more effort, but it's worth it for the enjoyment of licking the spatula!

Makes two 250-ml jars—

PRALINE

150 g (1 cup) whole hazelnuts, peeled
150 g (¾ cup) sugar
45 g (3 Tbsp) water

CHOCOLATE GANACHE

100 g (¾ cup) milk or dark chocolate
  chunks
150 g (⅔ cup) whipping cream

½ tsp vanilla extract or paste
pinch of salt

INGREDIENT NOTES

The recipe calls for hazelnuts, but almonds
will do just as well. For the chocolate we use
Valrhona Caraïbe callets, but you can use
any dark chocolate you like, cut into chunks.
Remember that the quality of chocolate you
use will ultimately affect the final taste.

A quick way to peel hazelnuts is to heat
them on a baking sheet in the oven at 350°F
(180°C) for about 5 minutes. Let them cool,
and then place them in a tea towel and rub to
remove the skins.

EQUIPMENT

You will need a food processor or a mini
chopper.

Chocolate Praline
PÂTE À TARTINER

TO MAKE THE PRALINE

1   Preheat your oven to 350°F (180°C). Spread the peeled
    hazelnuts on a baking sheet and roast in the oven for
    10 to 15 minutes, until golden brown. Set aside.

2   In a saucepan over medium heat, cook the sugar and
    water until golden brown or amber in colour.

3   When the sugar has reached the desired colour,
    remove from heat and stir in the hazelnuts.
    Immediately pour the caramelized nuts back onto
    the baking sheet. It's important to work quickly so
    you can spread the nuts while the sugar is still warm
    and soft. Set aside for about 15 minutes, until the
    sugar has hardened and cooled.

4   Break the candied nuts up into manageable chunks
    and place them in your food processor. Pulse until
    the praline is finely ground *(Photo A)*.

TO MAKE THE CHOCOLATE GANACHE

5   Slowly melt the chocolate over a double boiler or in
    a microwave on half power.

6   While the chocolate is melting, heat the cream in
    a saucepan until scalding (just before boiling). Pour
    the hot cream over the chocolate in two parts, using a
    spatula to mix well between each addition.

TO FINISH THE PÂTE À TARTINER

7   Stir the vanilla, salt, and ground praline into the
    chocolate ganache, then transfer the finished pâte à
    tartiner into jars or a container.

SERVING & STORAGE

This chocolate praline spread will keep in the refrigerator for up to two weeks. It gets a bit firm when chilled,
so you might find it easier to let it come to room
temperature before serving or briefly microwave it to
soften a bit.

Makes one 250-ml jar—

WHITE CHOCOLATE GANACHE

105 g (¾ cup) white chocolate chunks
55 g (¼ cup) whipping cream
pinch of salt
pinch of ground nutmeg

BLUEBERRY COMPOTE

**180 g (1⅓ cups) wild blueberries, fresh
   or frozen**
3 Tbsp water
1 Tbsp lemon juice
3 Tbsp sugar
pinch of salt

Blueberry White Chocolate
PÂTE À TARTINER

TO MAKE THE WHITE CHOCOLATE GANACHE

1 Slowly melt the white chocolate over a double boiler or in a microwave on half power. While the chocolate is melting, heat the cream, salt, and nutmeg in a saucepan until scalding (just before boiling).

2 Pour the hot cream over the chocolate in two parts, mixing well between each addition. Refrigerate for 20 to 30 minutes. The ganache should be chilled but not completely set.

3 Pour the partially set ganache into the bottom of your jar and refrigerate.

TO MAKE THE BLUEBERRY COMPOTE

4 Place the blueberries, water, and lemon juice in a small saucepan over medium heat. Mash and stir the blueberries until the mixture starts to boil around the sides of the pot.

5 Add the sugar and salt and turn the heat down to medium-low. Keeping the blueberries at a gentle boil and stirring occasionally, cook for 7 to 10 minutes, until the mixture has started to thicken.

6 Remove from heat and set aside until thickened and set. Give it an occasional stir as it cools.

7 Once the blueberry compote has set, spoon it into the jar over the ganache. Cover and refrigerate.

STORAGE

This spread will keep in the refrigerator for up to two weeks.

Tonka Bean
MILK JAM

There's something magical about the aroma of freshly grated tonka bean. These beans have a scent and flavour that is a bit difficult to pin down: some say it reminds them of vanilla; others detect cherries, cinnamon, or pepper, with a subtle smokiness. But for me, tonka beans have a totally unique flavour unlike anything I've ever had before. For a sensational flavour twist, in any recipe that calls for vanilla bean seeds, you can replace them with finely grated tonka bean.

PROCEDURE

1 Place all the ingredients in a saucepan and, whisking constantly, bring to a boil. Turn the heat down to low. Let simmer, uncovered, for about 1½ hours, whisking occasionally and skimming off any excess foam as needed. You'll know when it is done when the milk has reduced to about half its volume, thickened, and started to take on colour. The time that this takes will vary greatly depending on your stove, so keep an eye on it after the 1-hour mark (it can take up to 2 hours to reach the right consistency).

2 Once the milk jam is done, transfer it into jars and refrigerate. It will continue to thicken in the refrigerator as it chills.

STORAGE

This milk jam will keep in the refrigerator for up to two weeks.

Makes two 250-ml jars—

INGREDIENTS
500 g (2 cups) whole milk
500 g (2 cups) whipping cream
300 g (1½ cups) sugar
½ tsp fleur de sel (sea salt)
½ tonka bean, grated (about 1 tsp)

INGREDIENT NOTE
Although a bit tricky to find in stores, in Canada tonka beans are readily available online.

BAKED EGGS
Spanish-style

Serves 6—

ALMOND PESTO

small bunch of parsley (about ¾ cup),
    roughly chopped
25 g (¼ cup) sliced almonds or pine nuts
1 garlic clove
4 Tbsp olive oil
2 Tbsp champagne vinegar or white-
    wine vinegar
1 Tbsp water
⅛ tsp salt

EGGS

6 Tbsp almond pesto
75 g (3 cups loosely packed) fresh spinach,
    roughly chopped
175 g (¾ cup) cream
6 large eggs, at room temperature
6 slices ibérico or serrano ham,
    cut in half

FINISHING

3 plum tomatoes, diced
1 shallot, finely chopped
shaved manchego cheese (or parmesan),
    to taste
fleur de sel (sea salt)
freshly ground pepper
arugula *(optional)*
toast, to serve *(optional)*

EQUIPMENT

You will need a 10-inch round ovenproof
cast-iron pan or a 9-by-13-inch baking dish
(glass or ceramic). For individual servings,
use six ovenproof ramekins. If you use a cast-
iron pan, the eggs may cook a bit more quickly,
so keep a close eye on them in the oven.

*One of my friends makes a Spanish-style almond pesto tomato
salad that is to die for. I've adapted its beautiful flavours to
this egg dish that is perfect for brunch. I like to bake it in a
large dish; you can also easily use individual ramekins.*

    *The fresh tomatoes and shaved manchego cheese really pull
the dish together with their brightness. When I have arugula,
I also like to add a handful on top just before serving.*

TO MAKE THE ALMOND PESTO

1   Place all the pesto ingredients in a blender. Blend
on high until there are no large chunks. If the pesto
seems really thick, add another tablespoon of water
and blend again.

TO MAKE THE EGGS

2   Preheat your oven to 400°F (200°C). Butter the
baking dish or ramekins.

3   Mix 6 tablespoons of the pesto with the spinach.
Spread evenly over the bottom of the baking dish.

4   Pour the cream evenly over the spinach. Bake for
8 minutes. Remove the dish from the oven.

5   Gently crack the eggs into the dish and place pieces
of ham around the egg. Bake for 8 to 14 minutes,
until the whites are just cooked and the yolks are
still runny (it will take less time in a cast-iron pan).
There should still be a bit of jiggle when you shake
the pan. Let cool for 5 minutes.

6   While the eggs are cooling, toss the tomatoes, shallot,
and any leftover pesto together. After 5 minutes,
spoon the tomato mixture over the eggs and and
sprinkle with the shaved cheese, fleur de sel, and
pepper. If desired, serve with a handful of arugula
and toast.

SERVING

These eggs should be served as soon as they are ready.

Dimanche après-midi

SUNDAY AFTERNOON

SUNDAY IS THE ONE DAY OF THE WEEK that we hold sacred for family time. We set aside some time in the kitchen while keeping the rest of the schedule as light as possible. Although I'll sometimes make something a bit more involved, I generally go for simpler, more laid-back recipes on Sundays. The kids love getting in the kitchen with me, helping to crack eggs, stir, and whisk, all the while looking for their opportunity to sneak cookie batter or chocolate chunks. This chapter is filled with my favourite lazy Sunday recipes.

"SUNDAY CLEARS AWAY THE RUST OF THE WHOLE WEEK."
—JOSEPH ADDISON

Rosemary Gruyère
BRIOCHE LOAVES

Makes 2 loaves or 12 buns—

BRIOCHE DOUGH

30 g (2 Tbsp) whole milk

**13 g (1 Tbsp) fresh yeast, crumbled,
   or 8 g (2 tsp) active dry yeast**

250 g (1⅔ cups) all-purpose flour

30 g (2 Tbsp) sugar

1 tsp salt

3 large eggs, at room temperature

**145 g (⅔ cup) unsalted butter, cubed,
   at room temperature**

2 Tbsp finely chopped fresh rosemary

**100 g (⅔ cup) gruyère cheese, cut into
   2-cm cubes**

TOPPING

2–3 large egg yolks

finely chopped rosemary

fleur de sel (sea salt)

INGREDIENT NOTE

Using fresh herbs rather than dry will really give your brioche a nice flavour boost. Also, to finish the brioche, use fleur de sel (sea salt) rather than regular table salt: the iodine in table salt, when used as a finishing salt, can impart a pretty harsh taste. In contrast, fleur de sel has a gentle, soft flavour that is perfect for finishing off any savoury dish.

EQUIPMENT

You will need a stand mixer fitted with a dough-hook attachment, two 9-by-5-inch loaf pans, and two baking sheets. Alternatively, you can hand-shape the brioche dough into larger-sized buns and bake them directly on parchment-lined baking sheets.

I love brioche because of its satisfyingly rich and dense texture and slight sweetness. Although it takes a bit of time, making brioche dough is actually quite simple. The dough is quite versatile and may be left plain or transformed with savoury or sweet additions. This recipe makes loaves that can easily be separated into buns—the perfect accompaniment to any brunch or dinner. Rosemary is one of my favourite herbs and I always seem to have an abundance in my garden, but feel free to toss in any combination of fresh herbs and hard cheese.

A common mistake when making brioche is not mixing the dough for long enough. Although your mixer might hate you for it, make sure to mix it for the full 15 minutes to allow it to become completely smooth and elastic.

PROCEDURE

1   In a small bowl, warm the milk slightly so that it will activate the yeast (but not too hot or it will kill it). Add the yeast and stir *(see 'Yeast Facts,' page 39)*.

2   In a stand mixer bowl, combine the flour, sugar, and salt by hand. Make a well in the centre and add the 3 whole eggs and the yeast-and-milk mixture.

3   Fit the bowl on the stand mixer and, using the dough-hook attachment, mix on low speed until all the ingredients are well combined. Stop the mixer at least once to scrape down the sides.

4   On medium-low speed, gradually add the butter, a few cubes at a time. Once all the butter has been added *(Photo A, page 56)*, turn the mixer up to medium and continue mixing until the dough is smooth and shiny and has pulled away from the sides of the bowl. This should take 15 to 20 minutes. *Continued ›*

5 Add the rosemary and gruyère and mix until well dispersed through the dough.

6 Shape the dough into a ball and place it seam side down in the stand mixer bowl *(Photo B)*. Cover and let rise at room temperature for 1 hour, or until doubled in size. If your kitchen is quite chilly, go ahead and let it rise for an extra half hour.

7 Butter the loaf pans or spray them with vegetable oil. Set aside.

8 Punch down the dough and transfer it to a lightly floured surface. At this point the dough is ready to use, but it can also be wrapped in plastic wrap, lightly sprayed with oil, and stored in the refrigerator for up to 2 days or in the freezer for up to 1 week.

9 Using a knife or a bench scraper, divide the dough into 12 equal portions (about 50 g each).

10 Cup your hand over one portion of dough and, holding your hand in a claw shape, roll the dough in one spot using the pad of your thumb and the sides of your hand *(Photo C)*. This motion will shape your dough into a nice boule. The trick is to keep your surface floured to the right level: too much and there won't be enough traction to shape the dough; not enough and the dough will stick to the counter and tear.

11 In each loaf pan, place 6 rolled boules, seam side down so that their tops will be smooth, and space them out so they aren't touching (or touch as little as possible).

12 In a small bowl, whisk the egg yolks. Using a pastry brush, gently brush half of the yolk over the tops of the boules, making sure to cover them right to the edges *(Photo D)*. Set aside the remaining yolk.
Continued ›

13 To proof the boules, fill a pan with the hottest water you can get out of your tap (not boiling) and place it on the bottom rack of your oven. Place the loaf pans on a baking sheet, put them the oven, and close the oven door. Let the boules proof in the oven for about 1 to 1½ hours, until roughly doubled in size. Try not to open the oven door for the first hour as you want the steam to create a humid environment inside the oven.

14 Once proofed, remove the pan of water and the boules from the oven. Preheat your oven to 385°F (195°C).

15 While your oven is preheating, brush the boules with the remaining yolk and sprinkle with the rosemary and fleur de sel.

16 Place the loaf pans directly on the rack and bake for 15 to 18 minutes, until the boules are a deep golden brown.

SERVING & STORAGE

Brioche is best served warm, or at least the day it's baked. It will keep tolerably for up to three days in an airtight container.

CANDIED WALNUTS
50 g (¼ cup) sugar
¼ tsp ground cinnamon
¼ tsp salt
1 large egg white
2 tsp water
150 g (1½ cups) whole walnuts
10 carrot ribbons

FINANCIER CARROT CAKE
95 g (⅓ cup + 1 Tbsp) unsalted butter
150 g (1¼ cups) icing sugar
95 g (1 cup) almond flour (finely ground almonds)
50 g (⅓ cup) all-purpose flour
¼ tsp salt
¼ tsp ground ginger
¼ tsp ground cinnamon
150 g (about 5) large egg whites
1 tsp vanilla extract or paste
70 g (½ cup packed) grated carrot

Ingredients continued ›

INGREDIENT NOTES
The candied walnut recipe will make enough for two cakes, so you will have extra. They can be stored in an airtight container for up to six months, but they make such a delicious snack they are unlikely to last that long! I like to add carrot ribbons, long strips of carrot made with a vegetable peeler, to the candied walnut mixture to add a pop of colour to the top of the cake.

EQUIPMENT
You will need a baking sheet, an 8-inch cake pan, a stand mixer fitted with a paddle attachment, and a piping bag with a decorative piping tip *(optional)*.

Financier
CARROT CAKE

This is my take on an easy carrot cake. I like to use financier batter, made with almonds and beurre noisette—butter cooked until it turns a nutty golden brown—yielding a moist, spongy tea cake. It doesn't rise as much as a traditional cake, but the texture and flavour make up for that. If you want to turn this into a double-decker cake with icing inside, simply double the cake and frosting recipes. The candied nuts can be made ahead of time, but if you don't get there, you can sprinkle the cake with plain toasted walnuts instead.

TO MAKE THE CANDIED WALNUTS

1   Preheat your oven to 250°F (125°C). Line a baking sheet with parchment paper.

2   In a small bowl, combine the sugar, cinnamon, and salt.

3   In a separate bowl, whisk the egg white and water together until frothy. Add the walnuts and spiced sugar to the egg whites and mix to coat well. Stir in the carrot ribbons.

4   Spread the nuts out on the parchment paper, separating out the carrot ribbons to one side of the tray. Bake for 1 hour, or until golden brown, stirring every 15 minutes. Set aside to cool.

TO MAKE THE CAKE

5   Preheat your oven to 425°F (220°C). Line the cake pan with parchment paper and spray it with vegetable oil.

6   Make beurre noisette by melting the butter in a small saucepan over medium heat. Once fully melted, it will start to foam. Start whisking and continue to cook until the butter is a dark golden brown *(Photo A, page 60)* and has a nutty aroma. Set aside to cool.

7   Sift together the icing sugar, almond flour, all-purpose flour, and spices in a large bowl. Make a well in the centre and pour in the egg whites and vanilla. Mix until well combined. *Continued ›*

A

8   Add the cooled beurre noisette in two parts, whisking between each addition. Make sure to use a spatula to get it all out of the bowl—the dark brown sediment is loaded with a lovely nutty flavour that will make all the difference to your cake.

9   Add the grated carrot and mix until combined. Pour the batter into the prepared cake pan.

10 Bake for 25 to 28 minutes, until the cake is a dark golden brown around the edges and starting to brown on top. Allow the cake to cool in the pan, and then gently run a knife around the edge of the pan and flip the cake out. Make sure it is completely cool before frosting.

CREAM CHEESE FROSTING

115 g (½ cup) unsalted butter, at room temperature
225 g (1 cup) cream cheese, at room temperature
90 g (½ cup) sifted icing sugar
½ tsp vanilla extract or paste

INGREDIENT NOTE

The secret to a smooth and lump-free cream cheese frosting is to whip your butter and cream cheese separately and then combine them. It might seem like an unnecessary step, but it's quickly done and will give you a silky smooth frosting. It's very important that your butter and cream cheese be at room temperature before you whip them up.

TO MAKE THE CREAM CHEESE FROSTING

11 Place the butter in a stand mixer bowl and whip on medium speed for 2 minutes. Transfer to another bowl and set aside.

12 Place the cream cheese in the same bowl and whip on medium speed for 2 minutes. Add the whipped butter back in and whip together until well incorporated.

13 Turn the mixer off and add half of the icing sugar. Mix on low speed until well combined. Repeat with the remaining icing sugar. Add the vanilla, turn the mixer up to medium-high, and whip for another 30 seconds, or until light and fluffy. Scrape down the sides of the bowl as needed.

TO FINISH THE CAKE

14 Fill a piping bag with the cream cheese frosting. Pipe the frosting on top of the cake in a concentric circle or any decorative pattern. If you don't have a piping bag, spread it with a knife. Top with candied walnuts and pieces of carrot ribbon.

STORAGE

The cake will keep at room temperature for up to three days unfrosted or one day frosted.

Jacob at the cob oven, making Cheese & Herb Pan Bread (next page).

Cheese & Herb
PAN BREAD

Serves 12—

INGREDIENTS

1 Tbsp olive oil

1 small red onion, finely diced

290 g (2 cups) all-purpose flour

4 tsp baking powder

2 tsp dry mustard powder

1 tsp garlic powder

½ tsp salt

½ tsp ground black pepper

200 g (2 cups) grated sharp cheese

40 g (½ cup) grated parmesan cheese

2 Tbsp fresh parsley, finely chopped

2 Tbsp fresh chives, finely chopped

2 large eggs, separated

240 g (1 cup) buttermilk

80 g (⅓ cup) whole milk

180 g (¾ cup + 1 Tbsp) unsalted butter, melted and cooled

INGREDIENT NOTES

You can use any combination of sharp, firm cheeses to make up your 2 cups. My favourite is aged cheddar and gruyère.

EQUIPMENT

You will need a 9-inch cast-iron pan, a 9-inch springform pan (cheesecake pan), or a 9-inch square baking dish.

I first made this savoury quickbread in our wood-fired oven in our backyard. The delighted guests at our barbecue agreed that it was a hit. I like a simple mix of fresh herbs with lots of strong cheese in my batter, but you could easily use sundried tomatoes, olives, feta, or hot peppers to change the flavours. Of course, this bread is also delicious baked in a home oven.

PROCEDURE

1   Preheat your oven to 400°F (200°C). Spray the pan with vegetable oil.

2   In a frying pan over medium heat, heat the olive oil and sauté the red onion until softened and translucent. Remove from heat and set aside.

3   In a bowl, whisk together the flour, baking powder, mustard powder, garlic powder, salt, and black pepper. Mix in the cheeses, parsley, and chives. Set aside.

4   In a separate bowl, using a whisk or mixer, whisk the egg whites until soft peaks form.

5   In another bowl, combine the egg yolks, buttermilk, whole milk, cooled melted butter, and sautéed onion. Add the dry ingredients and mix until just combined. Gently fold in the beaten egg whites. Pour the batter into the prepared pan.

6   Bake for 35 to 40 minutes, until a golden brown and a toothpick comes out clean. Allow to cool for 15 minutes, then flip out onto a cutting board. Slice thickly and serve slightly warm.

STORAGE

This pan bread will keep at room temperature for up to four days. Reheat in the oven if desired.

Milk Chocolate Pecan
MUFFINS

Makes 12 muffins—

INGREDIENTS

290 g (2 cups) all-purpose flour
1 tsp baking powder
1 tsp salt
135 g (½ cup + 2 Tbsp) unsalted butter,
    at room temperature
150 g (¾ cup) sugar
2 large eggs
2 large egg whites
1 tsp vanilla paste or extract
180 g (¾ cup) whole milk
185 g (1 cup) milk chocolate chunks
65 g (½ cup) chopped pecans

EQUIPMENT

You will need a stand mixer fitted with a
paddle attachment and a 12-cavity muffin pan.

*Milk chocolate and pecans are a combination that never
gets old. These muffins are a bit sweet for breakfast, so I
make them more as a special afternoon treat. The batter is
good in the refrigerator for up to five days, so if you want
to double the recipe you can keep some batter to bake more
fresh muffins later in the week.*

PROCEDURE

1 Preheat your oven to 350°F (180°C). If you are not
   using paper muffin liners, spray the muffin pan with
   vegetable oil.

2 In a bowl, sift together the flour, baking powder, and
   salt. Set aside.

3 Place the butter and sugar in a stand mixer bowl.
   Cream on medium-high speed for 2 minutes, or
   until light and fluffy. Scrape down the sides of the
   bowl as needed.

4 Turn the mixer down to low speed and gradually
   add the whole eggs and egg whites in three parts.
   Scrape down the sides of the bowl between each
   addition. After all of the egg has been added, add
   the vanilla. Turn the mixer up to medium-high and
   mix for about 30 seconds more, until the butter and
   eggs are well incorporated and most of the lumps
   have disappeared.

5 Turn the mixer back down to low speed. Add the
   flour mixture in three parts alternating with the
   milk in two parts, beginning and ending with the
   dry mixture. Be sure to scrape down the sides of the
   bowl between each addition. *Continued ›*

6   Remove the bowl from the mixer and fold in the milk chocolate and pecans.

7   Using an ice cream scoop or a spoon, divide the batter evenly between the 12 muffin cups. Bake for 25 to 30 minutes, until a toothpick comes out clean or the centres of the muffins spring back to the touch. The tops of the muffins will be light in colour. Unmould while still hot and transfer to a cooling rack.

STORAGE

These muffins will keep at room temperature for up to three days. The unbaked batter will keep in the refrig-erator for up to five days.

GOUGÈRES

Gougères are made using pâte à choux (choux pastry), the foundation for many different pastries such as éclairs and chouquettes (cream puffs). Although pâte à choux usually features sweet fillings, the dough itself has almost no sugar and is just as delicious for savoury pastries. I call gougères 'cheesy little clouds' because of how light they are, and often find myself eating one after another without even thinking about it. They can be whipped up in no time, and after you pipe the dough you can even freeze them unbaked. Bake them from frozen for a quick snack or to serve as hors d'oeuvres for your dinner guests. Remember that these little beauties are best eaten warm out of the oven.

Makes about 12 gougères—

PÂTE À CHOUX

95 g (¼ cup + 2 Tbsp) skim milk
95 g (¼ cup + 2 Tbsp) water
90 g (¼ cup + 2 Tbsp) unsalted butter
½ tsp salt
½ tsp sugar
105 g (⅔ cup) all-purpose flour
3 large eggs

GOUGÈRES

50 g (⅓ cup) gruyère cheese, shredded, plus extra for sprinkling
2 tsp fresh thyme, finely chopped
½ tsp ground black pepper
1 large egg yolk, beaten

INGREDIENT NOTES

Gruyère is my favourite cheese to use in savoury baking. You can also use any other hard cheese, such as parmesan, asiago, or manchego.

EQUIPMENT

You will need a stand mixer fitted with a paddle attachment, two baking sheets, and a piping bag fitted with a large round tip *(optional)*.

TO MAKE THE PÂTE À CHOUX

1   Preheat the oven to 375°F (190°C). Line the baking sheets with parchment paper. If using a piping bag, set it up so it's ready to fill as soon as the dough is ready.

2   Place the skim milk, water, butter, salt, and sugar in a saucepan and bring to a simmer.

3   Turn the heat down to low, add the flour all at once, and begin stirring with a flat wooden spoon. The dough will form a mass and start pulling away from the sides of the pan. Stir vigorously without stopping for 2 to 3 minutes. The dough will darken a bit in colour and slightly dry out *(Photo A)*, which is what you want, as otherwise it may be too runny to pipe.

4   Immediately transfer the dough into a stand mixer bowl. With the mixer on medium-low speed, add the eggs one at time, mixing well between each addition. The dough should look like thick cake batter *(Photo B)*. Remove the bowl from the mixer. *Continued ›*

5   Fold in the cheese, thyme, and pepper. Your pâte à choux is now ready to pipe.

6   Immediately fill the piping bag with the pâte à choux. Hold the piping bag vertically with the tip ½ inch above the tray and pipe 2-inch circles onto the parchment. Try to keep the bag steady so that the dough falls continuously into the centre of each circle.

   Alternatively, use a spoon to drop dollops of dough onto the baking sheet. The final shape of your gougères will be less consistent, but they will be just as delicious.

7   Use your finger to gently run egg yolk over the top of each circle, making sure to smooth down any bumps *(Photo C)*.

8   Sprinkle grated gruyère over the tops of the gougères *(Photo D)*. Immediately bake for 30 minutes. Do not open the oven door during baking or your gougères will deflate. After 30 minutes, open the oven door for 10 to 15 seconds to let any built-up steam escape. Close it again and continue to bake for another 5 to 10 minutes, until you can feel that the outside of the dough has crisped up and it is a dark golden brown.

SERVING & STORAGE

Gougères are best eaten warm out of the oven. They will keep at room temperature for up to three days and can be briefly reheated before serving.

Triple Chocolate Chip
COOKIES

Makes 18 cookies—

INGREDIENTS

260 g (1¾ cups) all-purpose flour

½ tsp baking soda

½ tsp baking powder

1 tsp fleur de sel (sea salt)

140 g (⅔ cup) unsalted butter, at room temperature

160 g (1 cup firmly packed) dark brown sugar

115 g (½ cup + 1 Tbsp) granulated sugar

1 tsp vanilla paste or extract

1 large egg, at room temperature

30 g (¼ cup) cocoa nibs

75 g (½ cup) dark chocolate chunks

75 g (½ cup) milk chocolate chunks

EQUIPMENT

You will need a stand mixer fitted with a paddle attachment and two baking sheets.

Everyone is always looking for a good chocolate chip cookie recipe, which is perhaps the reason why this is by far our most requested recipe at the Bake Shop. Our good friends over at JACEK Chocolate Couture roast their own cocoa beans that they crush up into cocoa nibs. These have a unique flavour that goes well with Caramélia milk chocolate and Caraïbe dark chocolate, both superb-quality chocolates by Valrhona. Of course, not everyone has access to these types of chocolate, so feel free to use any products or combinations you like. Just remember—as always—it's all in the quality of chocolate you use!

PROCEDURE

1   Preheat your oven to 350°F (180°C). Line the baking sheets with parchment paper.

2   In a bowl, whisk together the flour, baking soda, baking powder, and fleur de sel. Set aside.

3   Place the butter in a stand mixer bowl. Cream on medium speed for 2 minutes, scraping down the sides of the bowl as needed. Add the sugars and vanilla. Cream for another 2 minutes, or until smooth, scraping down the sides of the bowl as needed. Add the egg and mix until light and fluffy.

4   Turn the mixer down to low, add the flour mixture, and mix until just combined. Remove the bowl from the mixer and fold in the cocoa nibs and chocolates.

5   Using an ice cream scoop, a spoon, or your hands, shape the dough into 1½- to 2-inch balls. Place the balls on the lined baking sheets about 3 inches apart.

6   Bake for 16 to 18 minutes, until the cookies are light golden brown and still a bit soft in the middle. Immediately transfer to a cooling rack.

STORAGE

These cookies will keep at room temperature for up to five days.

SHORTBREAD

325 g (2¼ cups) all-purpose flour
35 g (¼ cup) rice flour
½ tsp salt
240 g (1 cup + 2 Tbsp) unsalted butter,
　at room temperature
115 g (½ cup + 1 Tbsp) sugar
1 Tbsp finely ground Earl Grey tea leaves
1 tsp vanilla extract or paste

ICING

120 g (1 cup) icing sugar, sifted
2 Tbsp whole milk
½ tsp vanilla paste, or the seeds of half
　of a vanilla bean pod
Earl Grey tea leaves, for decoration

INGREDIENT NOTES

For most of our pastries at Duchess, we use
butter with a high fat content (82%–84%).
Shortbread is one of the few exceptions because, while high-fat butter is highly flavourful,
it doesn't hold its shape very well. For this
recipe it's best to use regular butter with a
lower fat content, that is, typical grocery-
store butter.

To get finely ground Earl Grey tea, simply
grind dried tea leaves with a mortar and
pestle or a spice grinder. For decoration,
using a variety with lavender or cornflowers is
especially pretty.

EQUIPMENT

You will need a stand mixer fitted with a
paddle attachment, two baking sheets, and a
2- to 3-inch round cookie cutter.

London Fog
SHORTBREAD

*Whether visiting with family or curling up with a cup of
tea and a good book, these are the perfect Sunday afternoon nibble. London Fog, a combination of vanilla, Earl
Grey tea, and milk, provides the flavour inspiration for this
version of the shortbread cookie. The inclusion of rice flour
gives the cookie a delicate crumb, and the unbaked dough
freezes nicely if you want to save some for a rainy day.*

TO MAKE THE SHORTBREAD

1　Line the baking sheets with parchment paper.

2　In a bowl, whisk together the all-purpose flour, rice
　flour, and salt. Set aside.

3　Place the butter and sugar in a stand mixer bowl.
　Cream on medium speed for 2 minutes, or until
　light and fluffy. Scrape down the sides of the bowl
　as needed. Add the ground Earl Grey tea and vanilla
　and mix again.

4　Add the flour mixture and mix on low speed until
　small pebbles form. Turn the mixer up to medium
　and mix until large pebbles form or the dough starts
　to come together *(Photo A, page 72)*. Stop the mixer
　and remove the bowl. Use your hands to shape the
　dough into a flattened ball *(Photo B, page 72)*.

5　On a lightly floured surface, roll out the dough to
　about ½ cm thick. Using a round cookie cutter, cut
　out cookies and gently place them about 2 inches
　apart on the lined baking sheets. Continue to re-roll
　dough scraps and cut out cookies until all the dough
　has been used. *Continued ›*

6 Place the baking sheets in the refrigerator or freezer for 15 to 20 minutes to chill the cookies prior to baking. You can bake them directly after rolling them, but they may spread a little or end up with more air bubbles.

7 While the unbaked cookies are chilling, preheat your oven to 275°F (135°C). Bake for 40 to 45 minutes, until the cookies are slightly golden but still quite pale in colour. Cool completely before icing.

TO MAKE THE ICING & FINISH THE COOKIES

8 Whisk together the icing sugar, milk, and vanilla paste or seeds. Dip each cooled cookie face down in the icing *(Photo C)*. Lay them flat, using your finger to catch any drips. Sprinkle with a few Earl Grey tea leaves and leave to set.

STORAGE

Shortbread will keep at room temperature for up to two weeks.

Madeleine, the family cat.

CHOCOLATE POTS

Serves 8—

CRÉMEUX

150 g (1 cup) dark chocolate chunks
190 g (¾ cup + 2 Tbsp) whipping cream
190 g (¾ cup) milk
80 g (about 4 large) egg yolks
50 g (¼ cup) sugar

ASSEMBLY

225 g (1 cup) whipping cream
2 Tbsp icing sugar
½ tsp vanilla extract or paste
berries, for decoration
icing sugar, for dusting

INGREDIENT NOTES

The quality of the chocolate you use is very noticeable in the final result. In this recipe I use dark Valrhona chocolate callets, whatever variety I happen to have.

EQUIPMENT

You will need a stand mixer fitted with a whisk attachment and an instant-read digital thermometer.

This light, not-so-sweet dessert is perfect for a chocolate craving fix. It falls somewhere between a crémeux (thick pudding) and a light mousse. It's really easy to make, has a wonderful texture, and always hits the spot when I need a little weekend pick-me-up. I'm a bit of a purist and usually like my chocolate mousse on its own, but sometimes I'll top it with fruit or crushed-up cookies.

TO MAKE THE CRÉMEUX

1   Slowly melt the chocolate over a double boiler or in a microwave on half power. Set aside.

2   In a saucepan, heat the cream and milk to scalding (just before boiling). Meanwhile, whisk together the yolks and sugar in a bowl.

3   Slowly pour the hot liquid over the yolk mixture while continuously whisking until all the liquid has been incorporated. Be careful not to add it too fast or the yolks will curdle and your mousse will be lumpy. If your bowl is slipping around on the counter while you're whisking, place a wet cloth under it.

4   Pour the mixture back into the saucepan and place over medium heat. Cook until the temperature reaches 28°C (82°F). Remove from heat.

5   Pour the hot mixture over the chocolate in three parts, mixing vigorously with a spatula between additions until smooth. Cover and set aside in the refrigerator to cool. *Continued ›*

TO ASSEMBLE THE CHOCOLATE POTS

6   Place the whipping cream, icing sugar, and vanilla in a stand mixer bowl. Using a whisk attachment, whip on medium-low speed until soft peaks form and the cream holds its shape when held up with a spoon.

7   Check the temperature of the crémeux. When it has cooled to about 8°C (45°F), add the whipped cream and whisk until there are no more lumps.

8   Pour or spoon the chocolate into cups, mugs, or little pots. Refrigerate for about 30 minutes, until set. Serve cold, topped with a few berries and a dusting of icing sugar.

STORAGE

Chocolate pots will keep in the refrigerator, covered, for up to four days.

Pear Blueberry Cheesecake
GALETTE

Serves 8—

INGREDIENTS

1 batch Easy Mixer Pie Dough, cold
   (page 80)
175 g (¾ cup) cream cheese, at room
   temperature
75 g (⅓ cup) unsalted butter, at room
   temperature
30 g (¼ cup) icing sugar
1 tsp freshly grated lemon zest
½ tsp vanilla extract or paste
2 Bartlett or Anjou pears, cored, sliced
   about ½ cm thick
150 g (1 cup) fresh or frozen blueberries
3 Tbsp sugar, plus extra for sprinkling
1 Tbsp cornstarch
2 tsp lemon juice
1 large egg white
1 tsp cream or milk

INGREDIENT NOTES

If you use frozen blueberries, do not thaw
them first.

EQUIPMENT

You will need a stand mixer fitted with a
paddle attachment and a baking sheet.

*A galette is a wonderfully rustic dessert that can be put
together with very little effort. I like to make this large
version at home, which I then slice into pieces, but individual ones are also easy to make. No need to fuss over perfect
edges—even if folded haphazardly the galette will turn out
nicely and delight everyone who gets to enjoy it.*

*Almost any pie filling can be turned into a galette, and
galettes are also great with savoury fillings. I love cream
cheese and blueberries, so for me this is a winning combination. I often switch the pears for nectarines, firm peaches,
or apples depending on what fruit I have that day.*

TO MAKE THE FILLING

1   Place the cream cheese and butter in a stand mixer
   bowl and whip on medium speed for 2 minutes.
   Turn the mixer off and add the icing sugar. Mix on
   low until well combined.

2   Add the lemon zest and vanilla, turn the mixer up to
   medium-high speed, and whip for another 30 seconds,
   or until light and fluffy. Scrape down the sides of
   the bowl as needed. Set aside.

TO ASSEMBLE THE GALETTE

3   Preheat your oven to 375°F (190°C). Line the
   baking sheet with parchment paper right up to the
   edges, to contain any filling that may bubble over
   during baking.

4   Lightly flour your work surface and place the cold
   dough in the middle. Lightly flour the top of the
   dough and, using a rolling pin, roll it from the centre
   outward, aiming to get it round. Keep rotating the
   dough as you roll it, lightly flouring the surface
   underneath as well as the top as needed to prevent
   it from sticking. Roll the dough out to about ½ cm
   thick. Use a knife or a pizza wheel to round out the
   edges. *Continued ›*

5   Place the circle on the lined baking sheet *(Photo A)*. The edges might hang over the sides a bit.

You can also make individual galettes by using a small bowl or saucer as a guide (about 6 inches in diameter) to cut 6 circles out of the pie dough with a sharp knife. You may need to re-roll the scraps to get all 6 circles. Continue as directed, dividing the fillings evenly.

6   Spread the cream cheese filling over the pie dough, leaving about 2 inches around the edge. Fan the pears evenly over the filling. If your pears are large, you may not need all of the slices.

7   Mix the blueberries, sugar, cornstarch, and lemon juice together in a bowl. If your blueberries are frozen, wait a minute or two to allow some of the sugar and cornstarch to dissolve. Scatter them over the pears *(Photo B)*. If there are dry ingredients left in the bottom of the bowl, make sure to sprinkle them on top as well.

8   Starting on one side of the galette, fold the pastry edge over towards the middle. Do this around the galette, overlapping each edge and leaving a circle open in the centre *(Photo C)*. Press down on the edges firmly to seal up the sides, to prevent too much liquid from escaping during baking.

9   Whisk together the egg white and cream to make egg wash and generously brush it over the pie dough. Sprinkle the entire galette generously with sugar *(Photo D). Continued ›*

10 Bake for 1 hour to 1 hour and 10 minutes, until the pastry is a golden brown and the filling in the centre is cooked and bubbling. Let the galette rest for at least 15 minutes before cutting. Serve warm or at room temperature.

STORAGE & SERVING

This galette will keep at room temperature for up to a day or in the refrigerator for up to three days. It can be reheated in the oven before serving, but it's best eaten freshly baked.

Don't skip the egg wash!

Although not completely necessary, brushing your pie dough with egg wash will make a huge difference in appearance. A golden, caramelized, flaky-looking crust is far more appealing than one that looks dull and pale. The trick to egg wash is to use one or two egg whites and about a teaspoon of cream or milk. The egg white will make the top of the crust shiny and glossy, and the milk will help brown it.

The best way to apply egg wash is to use a pastry brush with natural bristles. I find that with silicone nothing sticks and all of the egg wash slips off before I can get it onto the pie. If you don't have a pastry brush, the best way to spread egg wash is to use your fingers. It's a bit messy but does the trick.

Make sure to get the egg wash all over the pie dough, including in the cracks and on the edges. For sweet pies, a generous sprinkling of granulated sugar will caramelize slightly as it bakes and add to the overall texture of the finished dessert.

Easy Mixer
PIE DOUGH

Makes three 9-inch pie shells, or one covered or lattice-top pie plus an extra pie shell—

580 g (4 cups) all-purpose flour
225 g (1 cup) unsalted butter, in ½-inch
   cubes, cold
200 g (1 cup) vegetable shortening,
   in ½-inch cubes, cold
1 tsp salt
240 g (1 cup) ice water

EQUIPMENT

It's easiest to use a stand mixer fitted with a paddle attachment, but if you don't have one, you can mix the dough by hand using a pastry cutter or two knives.

This recipe will likely make more than you need for what you are baking. I always like to make the full recipe and keep the extra dough in my freezer ready to go for when I need to make a dessert in a pinch.

PROCEDURE

1 Place the flour, butter, shortening, and salt into a stand mixer bowl *(Photo A)*. Mix on low speed until the fats are in small chunks and the mixture looks a bit dry *(Photo B)*. This should only take 10 to 15 seconds. If you overmix you run the risk of turning your mixture into a dough, and then you'll have a difficult time incorporating all the water into it in the next step.

2 Add the ice water all at once and mix on medium speed until the dough just comes together *(Photo C)*. Some small lumps of fat should remain in the dough.

3 Shape the dough into 2 flattened balls *(Photo D)*. Wrap each ball in plastic wrap and refrigerate for at least 30 minutes, making sure the dough is fully chilled before rolling out. At this point the dough can be frozen. Let it thaw completely before using it, but when you roll it out, be sure it's still cold.

STORAGE

Pie dough can be stored in the refrigerator for up to two days or in the freezer for up to six months.

PIE DOUGH
Tips & Tricks

MAKING PIE DOUGH

- Use cold butter and shortening. When mixing the flour and fats together you want the fats to break down into small pieces but not totally disappear. This will be much easier to achieve if you make sure the fats are cold.
- Use ice-cold water.
- Don't overmix the dough. When you stop, you should still be able to see a few small lumps of fat and your dough should have a marbled appearance throughout. That's the secret to a flaky result!

BAKING A PIE

- When baking pies, always position your oven rack in the middle of the oven.
- Baking times may vary depending on your oven, the depth of your pie plate, and whether you're using disposable aluminum pie plates or glass/ceramic ones. All of our recipes are tested using glass pie plates, but even if that's what you're using too, you should use our baking times as a guideline only. Getting the perfect pie is really about checking the pastry during baking for the right colour. For a blind-baked shell, it should be light golden brown; for the top of a pie, it should be medium to darker golden brown.
- Place pies directly on the oven rack for baking rather than on a tray. If you're concerned about dripping, place a piece of aluminum foil on the rack below.
- Be careful not to overfill pies so that the filling doesn't boil over. *Continued ›*

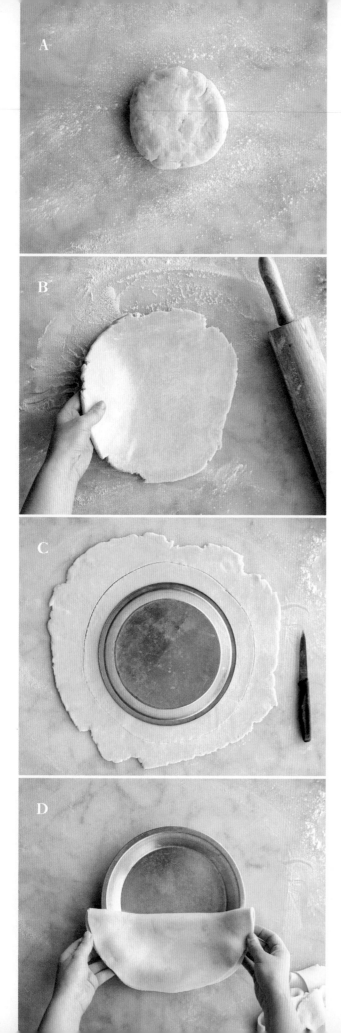

ROLLING OUT PIE DOUGH

1 Lightly flour your work surface and place the cold pie dough in the middle *(Photo A)*. Lightly flour the top of the dough and, using a rolling pin, roll the dough from the centre outward.

2 While rolling out your dough, keep rotating it, lightly flouring the surface under the dough as well as the top as needed to prevent it from sticking *(Photo B)*. Roll the dough out to about ¼ inch thick.

3 Flip the pie plate you will be using upside down onto the dough. Using a sharp knife, trace a circle 1 to 2 inches out from the edge of the pie plate *(Photo C)*.

4 Fold the circle of dough in half and transfer it to the pie plate, making sure it's nicely centred *(Photo D)*. Unfold the dough, and then, using your fingers, gently press it down to form the pie shell, leaving the extra dough hanging over the edge of the pie plate.

MAKING A BLIND-BAKED PIE SHELL

Blind-baking a pie shell means that you are fully baking the shell before filling it. We like to do it for really juicy fillings (such as strawberry rhubarb) or custard fillings (such as pumpkin) to make sure the crust on the bottom comes out crispy rather than soggy. For a pie that doesn't need to be baked (such as banana cream), a blind-baked shell is a necessity.

1   Working around the entire edge of the shell, snugly tuck the dough under itself, forming a thick rim around the edge of the plate *(Photo A)*.

2   Using the thumb of one hand, press the dough between the thumb and forefinger of the other hand, forming a crimped peak *(Photo B)*. Continue around the entire edge. Freeze the shell for at least 15 minutes.

3   Remove the shell from the freezer and brush the edges generously with egg wash (1 egg white whisked with 1 Tbsp cream).

4   Cut a large circle out of parchment paper—large enough to cover the bottom and sides of the shell—and line the shell with it. Fill the lined shell to about one-third full with dried beans, rice, or pie weights *(Photo C)*. This will help the shell hold its shape while it bakes.

5   Bake the shell at 375°F (190°C) for 30 to 35 minutes, until the edges are a light golden brown. Take it out of the oven and remove the parchment and weights. Using a fork, gently poke the bottom of the shell in a few places to make sure no air bubbles form *(Photo D)*. Place it back in the oven for another 5 minutes to finish baking.

Tourtière du Lac-Saint-Jean (page 105)

Je me souviens
I REMEMBER

MY FRANCO-ALBERTAN HEART—My ancestors came out West from Québec over a hundred years ago and today my family remains proudly Franco-Albertan. Growing up in an English-speaking province, my parents worked very hard to ensure that I was educated in French and that we spoke French at home. It took me until I was an adult to understand what a great gift my parents had given me and to take ownership of my French-Canadian roots. Although I spend the majority of my time surrounded by English, I wear my Franco-Albertan badge with great pride.

For us transplants from different provinces, over time we tend to lose touch with some of the colloquialisms, social nuances, and daily happenings of our provinces of origin. Still, the one thing we seem to cling to fiercely and celebrate passionately is food. Over shared meals, we continue to tell stories, gather with family and friends, and remember those who came before us. One of my greatest joys is sharing food traditions with family and friends. This chapter is my way of sharing my Francophone heritage with you.

"LA CULTURE D'UN PEUPLE, DANS SES TRADITIONS ET SES PENSÉES, DEMEURE ÉTERNELLE AU FIL DES GÉNÉRATIONS."
—DRISS REFFAS

Serves 8—

SAUCE

460 g (1½ cups) maple syrup
350 g (1½ cups) heavy cream

CAKE

165 g (1½ cups) cake flour
1 tsp baking powder
½ tsp salt
115 g (½ cup) unsalted butter, at room temperature
100 g (½ cup) sugar
½ tsp vanilla extract or paste
2 large eggs
ice cream or whipped cream, to serve

INGREDIENT NOTE

When buying maple syrup, make sure that it's grade A. This means that the syrup was tapped earlier in the season, is generally clearer and more delicate in taste, and has passed a quality test. Maple syrup comes in four different classifications: golden, amber, dark, and very dark. I prefer to use amber maple syrup for my baking, but if you like something a bit stronger with a deeper flavour, go ahead and use the dark or very dark.

EQUIPMENT

You will need a stand mixer fitted with a paddle attachment, eight ramekins, and a baking sheet.

When served warm out of the oven with a scoop of ice cream and a bit of extra sauce, pouding-chômeur is possibly one of the most sinful and satisfying desserts you will ever try. Originally this humble French-Canadian syrup cake was made with brown sugar, but the most recent versions use only pure, high-quality maple syrup. This makes the name 'chômeur' a bit ironic as it translates to 'unemployed,' and with the amount of maple syrup that's used, pouding-chômeur is far from something that someone saving their pennies would make.

PROCEDURE

1   Preheat your oven to 400°F (200°C). Butter or spray the ramekins with vegetable oil.

2   Place the maple syrup and heavy cream in a saucepan over medium heat. Bring to a boil and let it cook for about 5 minutes, stirring occasionally and watching that it doesn't boil over. Remove from heat and set aside.

3   Sift together the flour, baking powder, and salt. Set aside.

4   Place the butter and sugar in a stand mixer bowl. Cream on medium speed for 3 minutes, or until light and fluffy, scraping down the sides of the bowl as needed.

5   Add the vanilla and one of the eggs. Mix for 2 minutes. Scrape down the sides of the bowl, add the second egg, and mix for another 2 minutes, or until light and fluffy. *Continued ›*

6 Turn the mixer down to low speed, add the sifted flour mixture, and mix until just combined. Pour a small amount of sauce into each ramekin to cover the bottom. Using a spoon or an ice cream scoop, divide the batter among the ramekins (about 55 g per ramekin). Pour more sauce over the batter, filling each ramekin to just above half full. Reserve about a half cup of sauce to top off the desserts just before serving.

7 Place the ramekins on a baking sheet. Bake for 20 to 25 minutes, until just a golden brown and baked through.

8 Serve warm, topped with ice cream or fresh whipped cream and reserved sauce.

SERVING

Pouding-chômeur is best eaten warm out of the oven.

TARTE AU SUCRE
Maple Sugar Pie

Makes two 9-inch pies —

INGREDIENTS

2 blind-baked pie shells *(page 80)*

300 g (1½ cups firmly packed) golden
  brown sugar

150 g (¾ cup) granulated sugar

100 g (⅓ cup) maple syrup

600 g (2½ cups) whipping cream (35%)

200 g (¾ cup) whole milk

55 g (¼ cup) unsalted butter

1 large egg

50 g (¼ cup + 1 Tbsp) cornstarch

3 Tbsp water

EQUIPMENT

This recipe was tested using a 9-inch pie plate
(standard, not deep dish). If your pie plate is
a different size, you may need to adjust the
baking time accordingly.

The classic tarte au sucre recipe has many variations. Some recipes have a large amount of maple syrup and some don't use any at all. This filling has a little bit of maple syrup in it and a nice creamy texture. I love its simplicity and am happy to eat a slice unadorned.

PROCEDURE

1 Preheat your oven to 400°F (200°C).

2 In a saucepan, bring to a boil the brown sugar, granulated sugar, maple syrup, whipping cream, milk, and butter. Remove from heat.

3 In a medium bowl, whisk the egg. Very slowly drizzle the hot sugar mixture into the egg while continuing to whisk. If you add the liquid too quickly, the egg will curdle and your mixture will be lumpy. Once all of the liquid has been whisked in, set aside.

4 In a small bowl, mix together the cornstarch and water to dissolve. Add it to the pie filling and whisk until well combined.

5 Pour the filling carefully into the two pie shells, dividing it evenly. Bake for 5 minutes. Turn down the oven to 350°F (180°C) and bake for an additional 20 minutes, or until set.

STORAGE

Tarte au sucre will keep for up to four days in the refrigerator. It freezes tolerably well for up to three months.

TIRE SUR LA NEIGE

When I was growing up, eating maple taffy on snow (tire sur la neige) at our local sugar shack event (cabane à sucre) was the highlight of my year. We would head out as a family to our community festivities and my parents would let us loose for the day. I would immediately bolt to the tent that had the metal troughs filled with snow. I knew that the most magical snack was served there.

The maple-taffy-on-snow tent always had throngs of people crowding around the troughs. People would wait patiently with their popsicle sticks for the hot maple syrup to make its way around the tent and be poured on the snow. The crowds didn't deter me. I would crouch under the trough and, as soon as I saw the syrup headed our way, pop up in front of everyone, elbows out and stick ready. After rolling it greedily up on my stick, I would get back under the trough and eat my precious takings while waiting for the next pouring to come around.

My love for tire sur la neige still runs deep, and I found out that it's quite easy to enjoy it at home. We built ourselves a little trough of our own, but a large roasting pan will do the trick. On a nice winter's day, we make an afternoon of it, inviting friends and family over. It comes as no surprise to me that my children are at their happiest stick in hand and waiting for that hot syrup. Continued ›

For a group of 4 to 6 people, use a half can of maple syrup (about 1¼ cups), and for a larger group use a full can. When planning the activity, keep in mind that once the maple syrup is ready to go, you need to try to use it up within 15 to 20 minutes.

EQUIPMENT

You will need an instant-read thermometer and wooden popsicle sticks.

PROCEDURE

1   Fill a large, shallow roasting pan with fresh snow. Make sure to pack it down really well. If there's no fresh snow available, fill the bottom half of the pan with ice cubes and use a blender to grind more cubes into enough 'fresh snow' to cover the cubes.

2   Place the maple syrup in a saucepan and bring to a simmer on medium-low. When the syrup has reached 115°C (240°F), it's ready to be poured onto the snow. The amount of time it takes for the syrup to come to temperature can vary greatly depending on the amount being cooked (about 15 minutes for a half can and up to 30 minutes for a full can).

3   Pour the syrup in oval puddles on the snow, 2 to 3 tablespoons at a time, where it will soon firm up.

Advice on how to best enjoy tire sur la neige from eight-year-old me——

- Position yourself right up in front of a patch of fresh snow.
- Once the syrup is poured, let it hang out on the snow for 15 to 20 seconds.
- Starting at one end of the maple-syrup puddle, and using the flat side of the popsicle stick, dab the syrup around in the snow, making sure to pick up bits of it with the stick.
- Roll the syrup up gently onto the stick, making sure you get the whole puddle, while continuously dabbing at the snow to help it firm up. If it's too big a quantity to get it all in your mouth, lick it while holding the stick over a small cup to catch any falling *tire* to enjoy later.
- Savour every lick, and repeat until you feel you might burst!

TIRE SAINTE-CATHERINE
Pulled Molasses Taffy

Sister Marguerite Bourgeoys first made this candy in Québec in the 1650s to attract potential pupils to her new school in New France. She chose November 25 as the day she would make the taffy to honour the martyred Sainte-Catherine (the patron saint of unmarried and celibate women). It worked so well that every year on the same day she would repeat the tradition for all the local children. Soon the annual taffy-making became popular with unmarried women, who would give the candies (affectionately dubbed 'kisses') to potential suitors in order to show off their prowess in the kitchen.

Over time, this date became simply 'taffy day' for French-Canadians. I have fond memories of sitting at my desk in elementary school and having a piece of warm taffy placed on my desk for me to pull. It seemed like strenuous work, but the reward was oh so sweet as I sat on the school bus home and gobbled up the candies I had so laboriously wrapped in wax paper.

The flavour of this taffy is not unlike that of those poorly appreciated candies that children receive at Halloween, appropriately named Molasses Kisses. Yet I have never met a child who doesn't enjoy the fine tradition of pulling tire Sainte-Catherine!

Makes about 40 candies—

INGREDIENTS
200 g (1 cup + 2 Tbsp firmly packed)
  light brown sugar
160 g (½ cup) fancy molasses
60 g (¼ cup) water
55 g (¼ cup) unsalted butter
1 Tbsp maple syrup
½ tsp vanilla extract or paste
¼ tsp salt
¼ tsp baking soda

EQUIPMENT
You will need parchment or wax paper, an instant-read digital thermometer, a 9-by-13-inch pan, and a medium saucepan that can hold at least 1.5 litres. The taffy will expand as it's cooking and when baking soda is added to it, so it's important to have the right size of saucepan.

PROCEDURE
1 Butter the pan. Cut your wax paper or parchment into forty 3- to 4-inch squares. Set aside.

2 In a saucepan (at least 1.5 L) over medium-low heat, place all of the ingredients except the baking soda. Whisk to melt the butter and make sure everything is well incorporated.

3 Stirring occasionally, cook the taffy until it reaches 125°C (255°F). Turn off the heat and immediately incorporate the baking soda, being sure to mix it in well. The mixture will expand quite a bit, so don't be alarmed. *Continued ›*

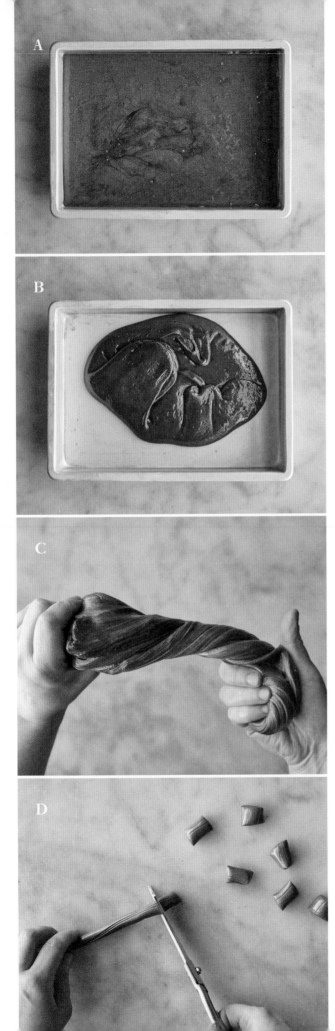

4 Pour the hot mixture into the buttered pan and set aside for a few minutes *(Photo A)*.

5 Once the taffy has started to cool around the edges, start pulling it from the edges of the pan towards the centre *(Photo B)*. If you let the sides of the pan cool too much, the edges will be much colder than the middle, and the taffy will be harder to work with.

6 Once all the taffy has cooled enough for you to handle it with your hands, it's time to pull. Cut it into 2 to 4 pieces to give to family and friends to pull.

7 Lightly butter your hands and begin pulling the taffy into lengths *(Photo C)*, folding it back over itself as you go. I like to give mine a twist after each pull, but taffy pulling can take on any form you'd like. If at any point it starts to really stick to your hands, you can roll it out a bit on the counter before continuing. Avoid adding too much butter to your hands as the taffy may start to split and be difficult to put back together.

8 Pull the taffy until it's lightened significantly in colour, but watch that it doesn't cool too much or it will be difficult to cut. When done, roll the taffy out into long ropes, and, using a clean pair of scissors, cut into 1- to 2-inch pieces *(Photo D)*.

9 Individually wrap each piece of taffy in parchment or wax paper.

STORAGE

The taffy will keep at room temperature, well wrapped, for two weeks.

Maple & Beer
BAKED HAM

Serves 12—

INGREDIENTS

1 Tbsp olive oil
1 garlic clove, minced
1 medium onion, finely chopped
    (about 1 cup)
1 can (355 ml) strong beer,
    such as porter or stout
240 g (1 cup) beef stock
170 g (½ cup) + 85 g (¼ cup) maple syrup
3 Tbsp Dijon mustard
3 whole cloves or ¼ tsp ground cloves
1 cinnamon stick
1 bay leaf
1 tsp ground black pepper
½ tsp ground coriander
½ tsp ground cumin
1 smoked pork shoulder (about 3–5 kg),
    bone in

This ham is a staple at our house for Easter. The sweetness from the maple syrup and the richness from the beer make it oh-so-flavourful, and while the ham is cooking, the house fills with the most marvellous aroma.

In my opinion, ham leftovers are the best. After we've eaten all the ham sandwiches we can manage, I cube the left-overs and portion and freeze them. These are great for making All-Day Breakfast Muffins (page 43) or Split-Pea Soup (page 101), or for throwing together a quick ham carbonara. The ham bone also makes a wonderful addition to any stock.

PROCEDURE

1 In a large pot over medium heat, heat the olive oil and sauté the garlic and onion until softened. Add the beer, beef stock, 170 g maple syrup, mustard, and spices. Bring to a boil, stirring well to make sure the mustard is dissolved.

2 Place the pork shoulder in the pot. Cover and let simmer on low for about 2 hours, until the ham is tender. Once the ham is done, remove it from the pot and remove any skin and excess membrane (and excess fat, if desired).

3 Place the pot back on medium-high heat and boil to reduce the liquid by about half. This should take 10 to 15 minutes. Once reduced, add the remaining 85 g maple syrup, stir, and set aside.

4 Preheat your oven to 400°F (200°C). Place the ham in a deep roasting pan. Baste with the reduced sauce. Bake in the oven for 15 to 20 minutes, basting frequently, until the ham is a dark golden in colour and has a caramelized glaze.

SERVING & STORAGE

Slice the ham and serve it warm or cold, topped with any remaining pan drippings if you like. Remove left-overs from the bone and save for making soup or stock. Ham will keep in the refrigerator for up to five days or in the freezer for up to six months.

Old-Fashioned
SPLIT-PEA SOUP

Serves 8—

INGREDIENTS

285 g (1¼ cups) dried split yellow peas
40 g (½ cup) diced celery
1 medium onion, finely chopped
3 L (about 12 cups) vegetable or chicken
   stock
1 ham bone
150 g (1 cup) diced carrots
15 g (¼ cup) finely chopped parsley
3 sprigs fresh thyme
1 bay leaf
salt and ground black pepper to taste
125 g (½ cup) diced ham or salted pork
crème fraîche or sour cream, to serve

From the time I was a small child, I had dreams of going to a real sugar shack in Québec. The idea of eating a big bowl of delicious warm split-pea soup and then gorging myself on maple syrup seemed irresistible.

It took me some trial and error before I came up with a recipe that could satisfy my craving. I found that by using the leftover ham bone from Easter dinner and adding cubes of maple-glazed ham, you can really pack a lot of flavour into a bowl. Whenever I eat a bowl of this soup, I imagine myself transported to a sugar shack in the woods.

PROCEDURE

1 Place the peas in a large bowl. Cover them with cold water, making sure that they are well immersed with at least an inch of water above them. Cover and let soak overnight (or for at least 8 hours) at room temperature.

2 Drain the peas. In a large saucepan, combine all the ingredients except the diced ham. Bring to a boil, and then turn down the heat to low. Simmer the soup with the lid off for 3 to 4 hours, until it has thickened slightly and the peas have softened. Adjust seasoning as needed.

3 Remove and discard the ham bone, thyme sprigs, bay leaf, and any large pieces of fat that may have separated from the bone. Add the diced ham and cook for a few minutes more, until the ham is heated through.

SERVING & STORAGE

Serve split-pea soup with a dollop of crème fraîche or sour cream. Leftover split-pea soup will keep in the refrigerator for up to five days. It can also be frozen for up to three months.

Sugar Shack
MAPLE BAKED BEANS

Serves 8—

INGREDIENTS

450 g (1 lb) dried white beans or navy beans
50 g (¼ cup) lard or vegetable oil
1 large onion, thinly sliced
170 g (½ cup) maple syrup
950 g (4 cups) water
2 Tbsp fancy molasses
1 Tbsp tomato paste
1 Tbsp Dijon mustard
1 tsp ground black pepper
1 tsp salt

EQUIPMENT

You will need an ovenproof pot with a lid.

These are my favourite baked beans, with a nice depth of flavour and just the right level of sweetness—perfect for any sugar shack party. They are a total snap to make— you just need to factor in the long baking time. Put them on before lunch so they can bake all day and be ready in time for dinner, or make them in advance to reheat and serve at your convenience. These can also be made in a slow cooker. In that case, cook on low for 8 to 9 hours or on high for 6 hours.

PROCEDURE

1   Preheat your oven to 350°F (180°C).

2   Place the beans in a large bowl. Cover them with cold water, making sure that they are well immersed with at least an inch of water above them. Cover and let them soak overnight (or for at least 8 hours) at room temperature.

3   Drain the beans in a colander, rinse them under cold water, and set aside.

4   In an ovenproof pot on the stove, melt the lard over medium heat. Add the sliced onions and sauté for a few minutes, until the onions have softened. Remove from heat.

5   Add the remaining ingredients to the pot along with the drained beans.

6   Cover and bake the beans in the oven for 6 to 8 hours, until tender. Stir every hour during cooking, adding more water (1 cup at a time) if they seem to be getting too dry.

SERVING & STORAGE

Serve hot. Leftover baked beans will keep in the refrigerator for up to five days. Gently reheat before serving.

TOURTIÈRE
du Lac-Saint-Jean

Serves 15 to 20—

INGREDIENTS

2 batches Easy Mixer Pie Dough,
  each made separately *(page 80)*
2.25 kg (5 lb) meat, cubed (beef, pork,
  chicken, or game)
2 large onions, diced
2 kg (8 cups) beef stock
1 bay leaf
2 Tbsp soy sauce
1 Tbsp Worcestershire sauce
1 Tbsp garlic powder
2 Tbsp onion powder
2 Tbsp dried parsley
2 tsp celery salt
1 tsp paprika
2½ Tbsp salt
1 Tbsp ground black pepper
4.5 kg (10 lb) potatoes, cut into 1-inch
  cubes
1 large egg white
1 tsp cream or milk

INGREDIENT NOTE

I like to use a mixture of stewing beef, chicken, and pork tenderloin, but feel free to use any combination of meat you like. If you would like to make your own beef stock from scratch, see page 139.

EQUIPMENT

You will need a 15-inch-long roasting pan (no lid), the same kind you would use to roast a turkey. This dish works fine in my inexpensive enamel pan.

Tourtière is a typically French-Canadian savoury meat pie. In Québec, it has easily a dozen regional variations. In my family, a traditional tourtière is shaped like a standard pie and made of ground pork and warm spices. When I first tried the version from the Saguenay–Lac-St-Jean region—lovingly made by Madame Hélène—I was blown away. I was surprised it was considered a tourtière because it bore no resemblance to the one I know. Baked in a large roasting pan, the meat is cut into large cubes and dispersed between layers of potatoes.

In the Lac-St-Jean region, Madame Hélène is famous for her tourtière, and I feel fortunate that she was kind enough to show me how to make this regional specialty. Although her original version uses onion soup mix and beef cubes, I wanted to challenge myself to come up with a 'from-scratch' version that was just as tasty—and I think I've come pretty close.

This is my favourite dish for large family gatherings. There is a bit of preparation involved (which can all be done the day before), and it takes several hours to bake, but once it's in the oven, the job is done. It will easily feed 15 people, and everyone is wowed when they see the large roasting pan stuffed to the brim with potatoes and meat. I serve it with Ketchup aux Fruits (page 263) and make sure there is plenty of beer on hand.

PROCEDURE

1 Mix the meat and onions together in a bowl. Cover and leave to marinate overnight in the refrigerator.

2 Place the beef stock and bay leaf in a pot over medium-high heat and bring to a boil. Let it boil to reduce it by half, until there are about 4 cups of stock left. Remove and discard the bay leaf, and stir in the soy sauce and Worcestershire sauce. Set aside to cool. *Continued ›*

3 In a small bowl, mix together the garlic powder, onion powder, parsley, celery salt, paprika, salt, and pepper. Set aside.

4 Preheat your oven to 425°F (220°C).

5 Roll out one batch of pie dough into a large circle or oval (depending on the shape of your roasting pan), to about ½ cm thick. Line the roasting pan with the dough, taking care to push it into every corner *(Photo A)*. Patch any holes with small pieces of dough. Let the excess dough hang over the sides of the dish.

6 Spread one-third of the potatoes over the bottom of the dish. Top with half of the meat and sprinkle over half of the powdered spice mix *(Photo B)*. Repeat the same layering again. Finish with a final layer of potatoes *(Photo C)*. It will seem like a lot of meat and potatoes to fit into the roasting pan. Even packing it down a bit I am sometimes left with a bit of extra potato that doesn't quite fit.

7 Roll out the second batch of pie dough in a large circle or oval and cover the tourtière with it *(Photo D)*. Using scissors, trim any excess dough around the sides, leaving about 1 inch overhanging. Working around the entire edge of the pan, snugly tuck the dough under itself to form a sealed rim *(Photo E)*. Using a fork or your fingers, crimp the dough to create a decorative edge.

8 Make a 1-inch vent hole in the centre of the dough and pour in the beef stock *(Photo F)*. This hole is very important to let steam out while the tourtière is baking.

9 Whisk together the egg white and cream and generously brush it over the edges and the top of the pie. *Continued ›*

10 Bake the tourtière for 1 hour at 425°F (220°C) *(Photo G)*. Cover the top loosely with aluminum foil, cutting a hole in the centre to let the steam escape *(Photo H)*. Turn your oven down to 350°F (180°C) and bake for another hour. Reduce the temperature to 275°F (135°C) and bake for another 4 to 5 hours.

Note: The total baking time for the tourtière is 6 to 8 hours, until the potatoes are soft. You can check this by poking a knife into the vent hole. There might still be lots of liquid bubbling up when it's ready to come out of the oven. Let the tourtière rest at room temperature for 20 to 30 minutes before serving. When you first cut into it, there might be a substantial amount of liquid. This is normal—as it starts to cool, it turns into a delicious gravy.

SERVING & STORAGE

This tourtière is best eaten warm out of the oven, but it makes for good leftovers for up to five days if kept in the refrigerator.

La belle France
BEAUTIFUL FRANCE

ON MY FATHER'S SIDE, the Courteau family came to Canada from France around 1685. Although it's been over four centuries, I've always felt a strong connection to France. I didn't get to visit the country until I was an adult. On my first trip, I fell in love with the place immediately. I am now a self-proclaimed Francophile and can think of nowhere else I'd rather go on holiday.

I've now been ten times and have no plans of stopping anytime soon, and even dream of someday owning a country cottage there. I often joke that I really should see other parts of the world, but for me, a perfect vacation is filled with cheese, wine, art, and of course, the finest pastries in the world. The recipes in this chapter are all inspired by some of my fondest memories during my travels in France.

"IN FRANCE, COOKING IS A SERIOUS ART FORM, AND A NATIONAL SPORT."
—JULIA CHILD

Makes one 8-inch tart—

VANILLA WHIPPED GANACHE
160 g (1¼ cups) white chocolate chunks
270 g (1¼ cups) whipping cream
110 g (½ cup) whipping cream, cold
1 tsp vanilla extract or paste

SABLÉ BRETON TART BASE
120 g (1 cup) cake flour
1¼ tsp baking powder
⅛ tsp salt
2 large egg yolks
80 g (⅓ cup + 1 Tbsp) sugar
¼ tsp vanilla extract or paste
90 g (⅓ cup + 1 Tbsp) unsalted butter,
    at room temperature

PISTACHIO BUTTER
100 g (1 cup) shelled pistachios
1 Tbsp honey
pinch of salt

ASSEMBLY
2 to 3 cups fresh strawberries
roughly chopped pistachios
strawberry flowers, for garnish (optional)

INGREDIENT NOTES
Choose the smallest strawberries you can find for maximum sweetness. Make sure the butter is at room temperature before starting.

EQUIPMENT
You will need a stand mixer fitted with a whisk attachment and a paddle attachment, a powerful food processor, an 8-inch round cake pan, and a piping bag fitted with a large plain round tip of your choice (#808 or #809).

TARTE AUX FRAISES
Strawberry Pistachio Tart

Gariguettes, fraises des bois, and ciflorettes are all wonderfully sweet French strawberry varieties. These little beauties are only in season in France for a few weeks in late spring. There is an explosion of strawberry desserts in pastry shops and on menus during this time as chefs scramble to make the most of the season's offerings. Using fruit that's in season is very important in the French culinary world, and it would be frowned upon to see a strawberry tart in a pastry case in January.

Strawberry and pistachio are a classic flavour combination. I love to eat pistachios on their own, but in desserts I find that their flavour often gets lost. This tart brings out the freshness of the strawberries while highlighting the nuttiness and texture of the pistachios, for just the right balance. I like making my own pistachio butter, but it can be tricky to do if you don't have a good food processor. If your food processor isn't up to the task, pistachio butter is readily available in specialty grocery stores.

TO MAKE THE WHIPPED GANACHE

1 Slowly melt the white chocolate over a double boiler or on half power in a microwave.

2 In a saucepan, heat the first measure of whipping cream until scalding (just before boiling). Pour the hot cream over the chocolate in three parts, mixing vigorously with a spatula between each addition until smooth.

3 Slowly whisk in the second measure of cream (cold) and the vanilla. The mixture will be liquid.

4 Let the ganache set in the refrigerator for at least 3 hours or overnight. It will thicken slightly but still be quite liquid. *Continued ›*

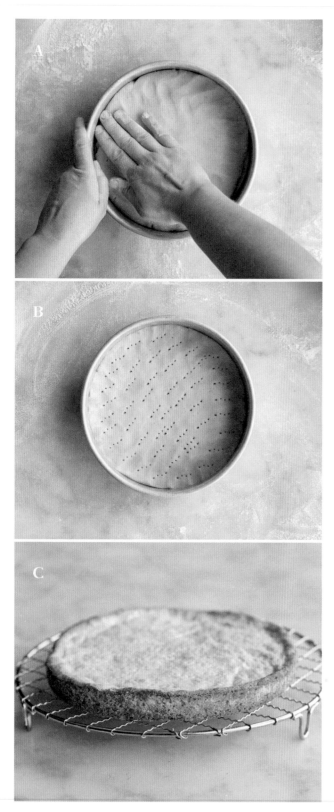

TO PREPARE THE TART BASE

5 Sift the cake flour, baking powder, and salt together and set aside.

6 Using a stand mixer fitted with a whisk attachment, whip the egg yolks and sugar on medium speed until thickened and lightened in colour. Add the vanilla and mix until well incorporated, scraping down the sides.

7 Switch to the paddle attachment. Add the sifted ingredients and butter and mix until just incorporated. Turn the dough onto a counter or table and bring it into a ball with your hands. Shape the ball into a flat circle, using a bit of flour if it's sticking.

8 Line the cake pan with parchment paper, and using your fingers, flatten the dough into the bottom *(Photo A)*. Using a fork, poke the dough all over to prevent large air bubbles from forming while it bakes *(Photo B)*. Refrigerate for at least 2 hours before baking.

9 When ready to bake, preheat your oven to 350°F (180°C). Bake for 25 to 30 minutes, until golden brown. Allow to cool slightly, and then gently flip the tart base out of the pan. Set aside and allow to cool completely at room temperature before assembling the tart *(Photos C & D)*.

TO MAKE THE PISTACHIO BUTTER

10 Preheat your oven to 350°F (180°C).

11 Spread the pistachios out on a baking tray. Roast them in the oven for 5 minutes, or until light golden brown.

12 Transfer the pistachios to a food processor. Blend for 6 minutes, stopping and scraping down the sides of the bowl as needed. *Continued ›*

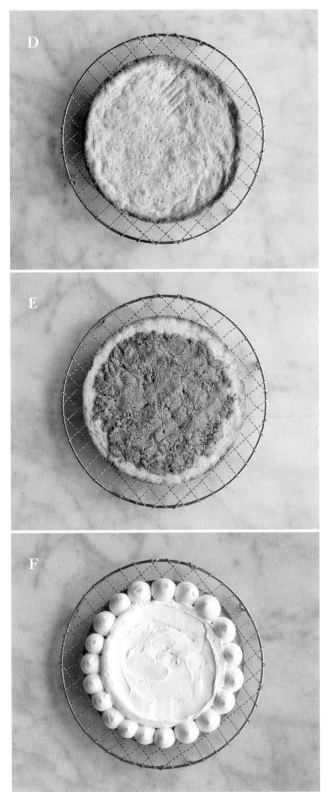

13 Add the honey and salt and continue to blend until it forms a smooth paste. This can take up to 15 minutes, depending on your food processor. If it's on the thick side, that's fine. Set aside at room temperature until ready to use.

TO ASSEMBLE THE TART

14 Spread the pistachio butter evenly over the sablé breton base *(Photo E)*.

15 Using a stand mixer fitted with a paddle attachment, whip up the ganache until soft peaks form. Keep a close eye on it: if it overwhips it will start to separate and end up grainy.

16 Fit a piping bag with a large plain round tip (#808 or #809) and fill it with whipped ganache. Pipe ganache in a circle over the pistachio butter, leaving about 1 inch around the edge. Pipe ganache dots about 1 inch wide by 1½ inches tall around the outside of the tart *(Photo F)*.

17 Artfully arrange the inside of the circle with fresh strawberries, pistachios, and strawberry flowers, if you like. Keep in the refrigerator until about 1 hour before serving.

STORAGE

This tart will keep well wrapped in the refrigerator for up to three days.

How to make
WHIPPED GANACHE
and why it's awesome

Makes 3 to 4 cups whipped ganache—

WHITE CHOCOLATE VERSION

160 g (1¼ cups) white chocolate chunks
270 g (1¼ cups) whipping cream
110 g (½ cup) whipping cream, cold

MILK CHOCOLATE VERSION

145 g (1 cup) milk chocolate chunks
270 g (1¼ cups) whipping cream
110 g (½ cup) whipping cream, cold

DARK CHOCOLATE VERSION

**130 g (¾ cup + 1 Tbsp) dark chocolate
chunks**
270 g (1¼ cups) whipping cream
110 g (½ cup) whipping cream, cold

THINGS TO KEEP IN MIND

I have provided the ingredients for whipped ganache for all three types of chocolate: white, milk, and dark. They differ only in the ratio of chocolate to cream, necessary because the various types of chocolate have different amounts of cocoa butter in them.

The ganache needs to sit in the refrigerator for a minimum of three hours before you can whip it up, as the chocolate needs that time to crystallize. If you try to whip it up before that, it may not come together.

I've never been a big fan of buttercream (except in macarons). It's usually too sweet for my taste, often has an unpleasant texture, and hardens like a rock when it gets cold. Enter whipped ganache—one of my favourite base recipes, as seen several times in this book. It's super simple to make, lighter than buttercream, has a lovely creamy texture, and pipes beautifully. It's also really flexible in how you flavour it—with extracts, fresh citrus zest, or spices, or even by steeping flavours into the cream. Use it to top cupcakes, tarts, fruit—the possibilities are endless!

PROCEDURE

1   Slowly melt the chocolate over a double boiler or on half power in a microwave. In a saucepan, heat the first measure of whipping cream until scalding (just before boiling).

2   Pour the hot cream over the chocolate in three parts, mixing well between each addition. After the first addition, the chocolate will 'break' and look grainy *(Photo A)*. Continue on with the second and third additions *(Photo B)*, making sure to mix vigorously after each. It will come together.

3   Slowly whisk in the second measure of cream (cold) *(Photo C)*. Cover and set aside in the refrigerator for at least 3 hours before whipping up.

4   Using a stand mixer fitted with a paddle attachment, whip until soft peaks form. Your whipped ganache is now ready to use.

BABA AU RHUM

Serves 8—

DOUGH

20 g (2 Tbsp) milk
20 g fresh yeast, crumbled, or
**   10 g (2½ tsp) active dry yeast**
110 g (about 2 large) eggs, at room
**   temperature**
145 g (1 cup) all-purpose flour
2 Tbsp sugar
½ tsp salt
90 g (⅓ cup + 1 Tbsp) unsalted butter,
**   softened and cubed**

SOAKING SYRUP

470 g (2 cups) water
250 g (1¼ cups) sugar
zest and juice of 1 orange
zest and juice of 1 lime
1½ tsp vanilla extract or paste
120 g (½ cup) rum

ASSEMBLY

300 g (1¼ cups) whipping cream
1 Tbsp icing sugar
1 tsp vanilla extract or paste

INGREDIENT NOTES

Make sure the eggs are at room temperature
before starting.

For the rum, a good-quality Jamaican
rum (such as Appleton) is ideal. In France,
they use *rhum agricole*, which is on the
lighter and fruitier side. Avoid using spiced
rum or white rum.

EQUIPMENT

You will need a stand mixer fitted with a
dough-hook attachment, a whisk attachment,
eight brioche moulds or a muffin pan or mini-
bundt pan, and a piping bag fitted with a star
tip *(optional)*.

*Baba au rhum, or simply 'baba,' is a yeasted cake that's
been soaked in rum syrup and topped with cream. One of
my absolute favourite desserts is French chef Cyril Lignac's
version of baba. I sometimes daydream of being magically
transported to his restaurant in Paris just to eat this dessert.
Of course, nothing can replace the experience of eating a
baba in a small Parisian bistro. This version is the closest
I've come to Cyril's, and it fits the bill when I'm craving a
good baba.*

*Baba dough is similar to brioche dough in that it uses
eggs and butter, but it tends to be a bit richer and have a
shorter proofing and resting time. The longer mixing time
for baba dough is very important as it helps to warm up
the dough and activate the yeast. Also, the babas need to
dry out at least overnight (but ideally 48 hours), so make
sure to factor that into your plans. They can actually be
made up to a week in advance and left out to dry, so if
you're having people over this is a great dessert that you
can prepare well in advance and finish relatively quickly
on the spot.*

TO MAKE THE DOUGH

1 If using dry yeast, warm the milk slightly in the
   microwave, sprinkle the yeast over the milk, and let
   stand for 5 minutes. Using your finger or a fork, mix
   well to form a thick paste *(see 'Yeast Facts,' page 39)*.

2 Crack the eggs into a small bowl and beat well with
   a fork. Transfer three-quarters of the egg into a
   stand mixer bowl. Add the milk/yeast paste, or if
   using fresh yeast, omit the milk and simply sprinkle
   it over the egg.

3 Add the flour, sugar, and salt and fit the bowl on the
   stand mixer. Using the dough-hook attachment, mix
   on low speed until completely combined, stopping
   the mixer at least once to scrape down the sides.
   The dough will look very dry.

4 Add the remainder of the egg and continue to mix
   on medium speed for 5 minutes. *Continued ›*

5 Turn the mixer down to medium-low speed and gradually add the butter, a few cubes at a time. Once all the butter has been added, turn the mixer up to medium. Continue mixing for 5 to 6 minutes, until the dough is smooth and shiny and starts slapping against the bowl and pulling away from the sides *(Photo A)*. If needed, stop the mixer to scrape down the sides of the bowl.

6 While the dough is mixing, spray the brioche moulds with vegetable oil and place them on a baking sheet.

7 Fill a large piping bag with the dough and cut about an inch off the tip. Divide the dough between the brioche moulds, using scissors to cut dough into each mould *(Photo B)*, distributing it as evenly as possible.

TO PROOF THE BABAS

8 Fill a pan with the hottest water you can get out of your tap (not boiling) and place it on the bottom rack of your oven. Place the babas in the oven, close the oven door, and let them proof for about 45 minutes. Do not open the oven door during proofing as you want the steam to create a humid environment inside the oven.

9 Once proofed *(Photo C)*, remove the pan of water and the babas from the oven. Preheat your oven to 375°F (190°C).

10 Bake the babas for 20 minutes. Unmould them, place them directly on the baking sheet, and bake for an additional 5 minutes. They should be a dark golden brown and feel hard to the touch. Set aside to cool.

Note: Ideally, leave babas out to dry at room temperature for at least 48 hours. This will prepare them for soaking up the maximum amount of delicious syrup. If you're pressed for time, they can be soaked as soon as they are cool, but the depth of flavour and the texture won't be the same. *Continued ›*

11 Bring the water and sugar to a boil over medium heat. Add the orange and lime zest and juice, vanilla, and rum. Turn the heat down, simmer for 20 minutes, and strain. The syrup will keep for up to 48 hours in the refrigerator.

TO DIP AND FINISH THE BABAS

12 When ready to serve the babas, warm the syrup in a saucepan that will fit 2 or 3 babas side by side. Remove from heat.

13 Dunk the babas in the warm syrup and let them soak for 4 to 5 minutes (a few minutes per side), until they feel spongy and heavy. The majority of the syrup will be absorbed from the porous bottom rather than the smooth top, but do roll them around to make sure that all sides are soaked.

14 Remove the babas from the syrup and place them upside down to drip dry on a cooling rack placed over a baking sheet. Cool for 5 to 10 minutes.

15 In a stand mixer bowl, place the whipping cream, icing sugar, and vanilla. Mix on low speed until soft peaks start to form. This can take up to 10 minutes.

16 Turn the speed up to medium-high and whip until stiff peaks form. Keep a close eye on it: if it over-whips it will start to separate and end up grainy.

17 Using a spoon or a piping bag fitted with a star tip, place a generous dollop of whipped cream in the centre of each baba. Serve immediately.

SERVING & STORAGE

Babas are best eaten as soon as they are finished. Dipped babas will keep refrigerated for 24 hours. Finish with the whipped cream when ready to serve.

PAIN D'ÉPICES CHAUD
Warm Gingerbread Cake

Serves 12—

CAKE

340 g (2⅓ cups) all-purpose flour
1½ tsp baking soda
3 tsp ground cinnamon
1 tsp ground ginger
½ tsp ground cloves
½ tsp ground star anise
½ tsp salt
220 g (1¼ cups firmly packed) dark brown
   sugar
200 g (⅔ cup) fancy molasses
140 g (⅓ cup + 2 Tbsp) liquid honey
210 g (1 cup) vegetable oil
2 large eggs
335 g (1⅓ cups) boiling water
zest of 1 lemon

SAUCE

115 g (½ cup) unsalted butter
150 g (¾ cup firmly packed) dark brown
   sugar
120 g (½ cup) whipping cream
1 tsp vanilla extract or paste
2 Tbsp calvados *(optional)*
vanilla ice cream, to serve

EQUIPMENT

You will need a stand mixer fitted with
a paddle attachment and a 9-by-13-inch
baking dish.

If you're ever driving the cider route in Normandy, there's a charming little restaurant in Cambremer called Au P'tit Normand that is a nice place to stop for lunch. Their warm pain d'épices (gingerbread) in calvados caramel sauce is the perfect comfort dessert. When I asked the owner about it, she replied, 'Oh, I just threw it together. It's just a standard pain d'épices—nothing special.' Well, for me, it was pretty special, and this is my homage to it.

TO MAKE THE CAKE

1   Preheat your oven to 350°F (180°C). Spray the baking dish with vegetable oil and line it with parchment paper. Put a kettle on to boil.

2   Sift together the flour, baking soda, spices, and salt and set aside.

3   Place the brown sugar, molasses, and honey in a stand mixer bowl. Mix on medium speed for about 1 minute. Scrape down the sides of the bowl.

4   With the mixer on low speed, slowly add the oil. Once incorporated, scrape down the sides of the bowl. Turn the mixer up to medium and mix for 1 minute.

5   Add the eggs and mix until smooth and well incorporated.

6   Turn the mixer down to low speed and add the dry ingredients and the boiling water, alternating three parts dry with two parts water and beginning and ending with the dry. Scrape down the bowl between each addition. Add the lemon zest and mix until just combined. *Continued ›*

7 Pour the batter into the prepared baking dish. Bake for 35 to 40 minutes, until a toothpick inserted in the centre comes out clean.

8 Melt the butter in a saucepan over medium heat. Add the brown sugar and cook until dissolved. Slowly pour in the whipping cream and continue to cook, whisking, until the sauce thickens slightly. Remove from heat and whisk in the vanilla and calvados if using.

9 To serve the pain d'épices, cut out pieces while still warm and top generously with warm sauce. Serve with vanilla ice cream.

STORAGE & SERVING

This gingerbread will keep at room temperature for up to five days. The sauce can be kept in the refrigerator for up to four days. Reheat both before serving.

Enjoying a castle in Alsace (top); the apple harvest in Normandy (bottom).

MERVEILLEUX

Serves 10 to 12—

MERINGUES
60 g (⅓ cup) dark chocolate chunks
90 g (about 3 large) egg whites
125 g (⅔ cup) sugar
pinch of salt
1 tsp vanilla extract or paste

WHIPPED CREAM
460 g (2 cups) whipping cream
30 g (¼ cup) icing sugar
½ tsp vanilla extract or paste

ASSEMBLY
140 g (1 cup) good-quality dark chocolate,
  finely chopped

INGREDIENT NOTES
Using good-quality chocolate for rolling your
merveilleux makes all the difference. I use
Valrhona chocolate that I finely chop myself.
If you want an easier, more aesthetically
pleasing option, you can always buy chocolate
shavings from a grocery store, but you will
be compromising on quality. You can also
make your own chocolate shavings by using a
vegetable peeler on a large block of chocolate,
but again, it's difficult to find good-quality
chocolate in larger blocks.

EQUIPMENT
You will need a stand mixer fitted with a
whisk attachment, a paddle attachment, an
instant-read digital thermometer, two baking
sheets, and a piping bag fitted with a large
round tip *(optional)*.

*The merveilleux, essentially two meringues sandwiched and
encased with cream, has been around since the eighteenth
century. It lends itself to a myriad of flavour variations,
and entire pastry shops in France are devoted to it. These
little desserts are messy to eat, and although you can eat
them with your hands—as I often do in Paris when I don't
want to wait until I get back to the hotel—I do recommend
a plate and fork.*

*The merveilleux is rolled around in a dry topping that
sticks to the whipped cream. Any crushed nuts, chopped
chocolate, shredded coconut, sprinkles, or even cake crumbs
are great for this.*

TO MAKE THE MERINGUES

1 Line the two baking sheets with parchment paper
  and set up your piping bag so it's ready to be filled
  (if using). Preheat your oven to 200°F (95°C).

2 Slowly melt the chocolate over a double boiler or in
  a microwave on half power. Set aside.

3 In a stand mixer bowl fitted over a double boiler,
  heat the egg whites, sugar, and salt over medium
  heat, whisking often, until the mixture reaches 54°C
  (128°F).

4 Remove from heat, fit the bowl to your stand mixer,
  and, using the whisk attachment, whip on medium-
  low speed until soft peaks start to form. Turn the
  mixer up to medium-high and continue to whip
  until stiff, glossy peaks form. Add the vanilla and
  whip until just incorporated.

5 By hand, gently fold in the melted chocolate, barely
  mixing it in to create pretty swirls *(Photo A, page
  126)*. At this stage, it's important to work quickly.
  Continued ›

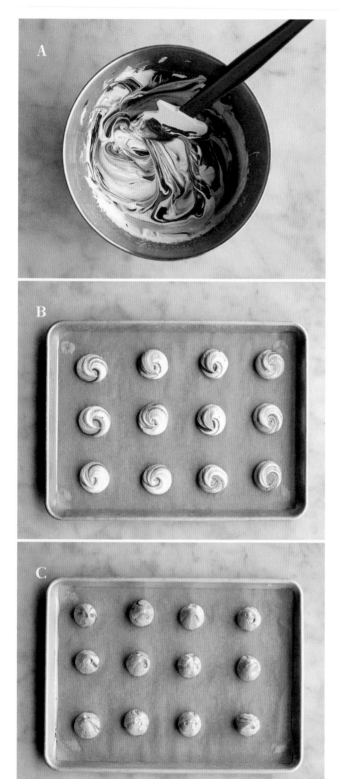

6 Fill the prepared piping bag with the meringue. Pipe twelve 3-inch circles onto a lined baking sheet, making sure to leave space between each *(Photo B)*. Alternatively, use a spoon to drop dollops of meringue on the baking sheet, flattening them a bit with the back of a spoon. The final shape of your merveilleux will be less consistent, but they will be just as delicious.

7 On the second lined baking sheet, pipe 12 taller meringue mounds, about the same width *(Photo C)*. The circles will be the bases and the mounds will be the tops.

8 Bake for 1½ hours, or until firm and dry. Do not open the oven door in the first hour of baking. When done, turn off the oven and let the meringues cool completely inside.

TO MAKE THE WHIPPED CREAM

9 Place the whipping cream, icing sugar, and vanilla in a stand mixer bowl. Using the whisk attachment, whip on medium-low speed until soft peaks begin to form. Turn the speed up to medium-high and whip until stiff peaks form. This process, which can take 5 to 10 minutes, builds small air bubbles in the whipped cream to give it good stability.

10 Keeping a close eye on the cream, turn the speed up to high. Mix until the cream looks very thick and almost overwhipped, as if it's on the verge of separating. It needs to be very stiff in order to hold its shape around the meringues. Be careful not to go too far or it will completely separate and turn to butter. *Continued ›*

126

TO FINISH THE MERVEILLEUX

11 Place a large dollop of whipped cream on each meringue base. Top with the taller meringues and push down gently but firmly so a bit of cream comes out the sides *(Photo D)*.

12 Hold each meringue by the base. Using an offset spatula or a butter knife, generously ice the meringues with the remaining whipped cream, working from bottom to top and making sure that each meringue is entirely covered *(Photo E)*.

13 Roll each covered meringue around in the chopped chocolate to coat well *(Photo F)*. Transfer the merveilleux to individual serving plates or small bowls and serve immediately.

SERVING & STORAGE

Before they are iced, meringues will keep well sealed at room temperature for up to a week. Once assembled, merveilleux are best served immediately, but they can be kept in the refrigerator for up to four hours.

GREEN CHAUD
Chartreuse Hot Chocolate

Makes 4 small cups—

INGREDIENTS
70 g (½ cup) dark chocolate chunks
2 tsp cocoa powder
2 tsp sugar
350 g (1½ cups) whole milk
60 ml (¼ cup) green chartreuse
freshly whipped cream, unsweetened

INGREDIENT NOTE
It is best to use a good-quality dark chocolate.
My preference is 70% Valrhona Guanaja, but
anything over 60% will do.

This hot drink, essentially a hot chocolate with green chartreuse (a herbaceous liqueur), is very popular as an après-ski cocktail in the French alps. The key to a good green chaud is to use dark chocolate and to make sure the drink doesn't come out too sweet.

PROCEDURE
1   In a medium bowl, slowly melt the chocolate over a double boiler or on half power in a microwave. Once completely melted, whisk in the cocoa powder and sugar.

2   In a saucepan, heat the milk. Keeping the milk hot, pour about ¼ cup of it over the chocolate and mix vigorously. Repeat with another ¼ cup milk. Drizzle in the remainder while whisking constantly.

3   Pour about 1 Tbsp of chartreuse in the bottom of each of 4 small mugs. Top with hot chocolate and a dollop of softly whipped cream. Serve immediately.

How to make super-silky-smooth whipped cream

When I was in junior high, my method for making whipped cream was very different from today. I would place my bowl and beaters in the freezer (I read this in one of my mother's baking books), whip the cream on high speed to within an inch of its life, and then feel very smug. I realize now that the result was really thick and chunky—that is, close to splitting.

The true secret is to whip it on low speed for a really long time (and no need to place your bowl or beaters in the freezer). This way you build lots of small air bubbles, resulting in a thick, creamy, smooth, and stable whipped cream. When you whip it on high quickly it builds fewer and larger air bubbles, giving you an airier, less smooth whipped cream that won't hold its shape for as long.

To whip cream, use your stand mixer with a whisk attachment and set it to medium-low. Depending on how much you're whipping, it can take up to 10 minutes. Keep an eye on it because it can overwhip quite easily, and suddenly you'll find yourself with butter.

CHAUSSONS AUX POMMES
Apple Turnovers

Makes 8 chaussons—

INGREDIENTS

400 g (3 or 4 small) apples, Granny Smith or Honeycrisp
60 g (¼ cup) water
50 g (⅓ cup firmly packed) dark brown sugar
30 g (2 Tbsp) unsalted butter
1 tsp vanilla extract or paste
¾ tsp ground cinnamon
¼ tsp ground ginger
1 package frozen puff pastry (2 sheets), each sheet about 10 inches square
1 Tbsp brandy or calvados
2 large egg yolks, beaten
sugar, for topping

INGREDIENT NOTE

If you are comfortable making your own puff pastry, feel free to do so. A much faster option is to buy pre-made frozen puff pastry. Make sure you look for one that's all butter—it's a bit pricier, but worth it for the quality and flavour. See page 170 for tips on how to work with puff pastry.

EQUIPMENT

You will need two baking sheets.

At 24 years old, I went overseas for the first time. Our first stop was Paris. Bleary-eyed and jetlagged, we checked into our hotel late at night with little awareness of our surroundings. The next morning when we left our hotel, we found ourselves in the most charming neighbourhood (Le Marais) and across the street from a little bakery.

We bought chaussons aux pommes, still warm out of the oven, and ate them as we walked towards Notre Dame Cathedral. I was sure I'd never tasted anything so delicious—and for the first time understood what it's like to really taste butter! Ever since, whenever I travel to Paris I always buy a chausson aux pommes for my first breakfast.

Traditionally, chaussons aux pommes are made using croissant dough, but that's pretty tricky to make at home. I find that with good-quality store-bought frozen puff pastry, you can make a very delicious version in your home kitchen.

TO PREPARE THE APPLE FILLING

1   Peel, core, and dice the apples into 1- to 2-cm pieces *(see tips, page 133)*. In a saucepan, combine all of the ingredients except the brandy, puff pastry, and egg yolks. Sauté over low heat for 25 to 30 minutes, until the apples are very soft, stirring every 5 minutes or so.

2   Once the apples have softened, turn the heat up to medium. Add the brandy and continue to cook until most of the liquid has evaporated. This should take less than 1 minute. Set the apples aside to cool, and then place them in the refrigerator. The apple filling needs to be completely cool before filling the puff pastry.

TO ROLL, FILL, AND BAKE THE CHAUSSONS

3   Line the baking sheets with parchment paper. Take the puff pastry out of the freezer and leave it on the counter to defrost. This should take 15 to 20 minutes. Make sure it is still cold when you start working with it. *Continued ›*

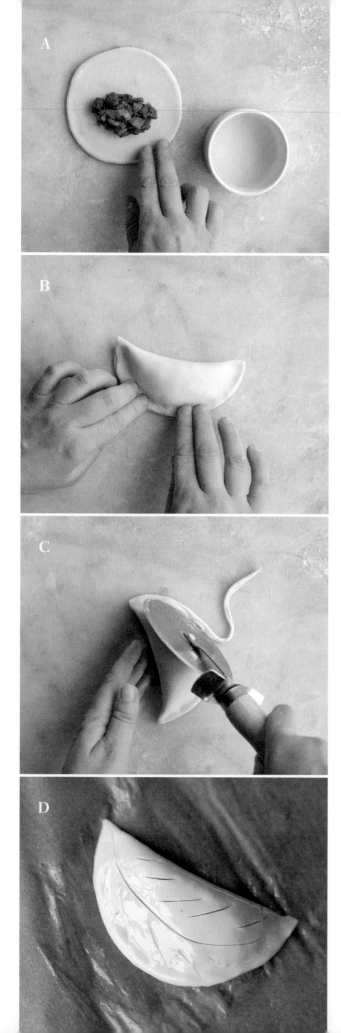

A

B

C

D

4 Once thawed, on a lightly floured surface, roll out each sheet of puff pastry slightly to make it smooth. Using a small bowl or lid 4 to 5 inches wide (about the size of a yogurt lid), cut out 4 circles per sheet.

5 Place 1½ to 2 Tbsp of apple filling in the centre of a circle. Using your finger, dab a bit of water around the edges *(Photo A)*. Fold the circle over to make a half-moon shape. Using your fingers, press down on the seam edge to seal well *(Photo B)*. With a pizza wheel (best option) or a sharp paring knife, trim the edge of the puff pastry to create a clean line *(Photo C)*. Avoid using a fork to crimp the edges as this will prevent the pastry from puffing out as it bakes. Save the scraps to make Easy Puff Pastry Cheese Twists *(page 171)*.

6 Transfer the chaussons to a lined baking sheet. Using a pastry brush or your fingers, gently brush egg yolk over the whole of each chausson.

7 Chill in the refrigerator for about 15 minutes. While the chaussons are chilling, preheat your oven to 375°F (190°C).

8 When the chaussons are cold, brush them with another layer of egg yolk. Using a small, sharp paring knife, score each chausson with a half-moon shape from corner to corner, making sure not to cut all the way through the dough. Score small diagonal lines on each side of the half-moon to create a leaf pattern, again not cutting all the way through *(Photo D)*. Sprinkle generously with sugar.

9 Bake for 30 to 35 minutes, until the pastry is a deep golden brown. Don't be alarmed if yolk that may have baked around the edges gets quite dark. After the chaussons have cooled to the touch, remove them from the parchment, cutting off any dark yolk drippings. Serve warm for maximum enjoyment!

SERVING & STORAGE

Chaussons aux pommes are best eaten the day they are baked. They will keep at room temperature for up to three days.

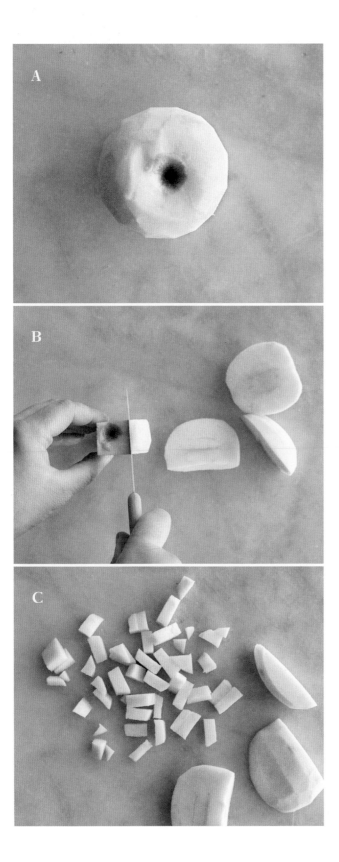

A

B

C

How to core & cut an apple

I'm not one for useless kitchen gadgets, and the apple corer is high on my list of gadgets that are hard to use and don't get the job done right. When I push it through I tend to miss half of the seeds and core, and then I'm stuck having to cut my apple in half and core it by hand anyway. And when apple gets stuck in the corer, getting it out is a pain.

My favourite way to core and cut an apple is to take my peeled apple *(Photo A)* and cut four sides off around the core in a square *(Photo B)*. That way I'm left with the core I can easily discard and four flat pieces I can slice or dice as I like *(Photo C)*.

If you do have an apple corer kicking around and are an avid pie maker, don't get rid of it. It does serve one useful purpose, and that's to cut the perfect vent hole in the top of a covered pie!

HOMEMADE
BUTTER

The yield of finished butter can vary from anywhere between 375 g and 450 g—

PLAIN SALTED BUTTER

1 L heavy cream (35%–55% fat)
¾ tsp fleur de sel (sea salt) for every
375 g finished butter

INGREDIENT NOTE
The higher-fat cream you can find, the better your butter will be.

EQUIPMENT
You will need a stand mixer with a whisk attachment and paddle attachment.

See next page for flavour variations ›

Because virtually no one makes their own butter, it is easy to assume that's because it's too difficult. In fact it is actually quite simple to do—and you get the added benefit of having leftover buttermilk that you can freeze for future baking.

I call my homemade butter 'eating butter,' which means that I don't use it for baking but rather to slather on bread, pancakes, warm potatoes, or anything that needs that extra deliciousness. Flavoured butters make great Christmas gifts. I have a few wooden butter moulds and stamps that I bought in France that are really charming; another great option is to simply roll your butter into a log shape and then cut it into rounds.

The trick to making homemade butter successfully is to use good-quality high-fat cream as your base. We have a local dairy producer that makes a heavy cream that's 52% butterfat, ideal for butter making. In a grocery store, the highest percentage butterfat you can usually find is 35%. You can certainly make good butter with it, but it will be considerably lighter in colour and won't be as flavourful.

PROCEDURE

1   Place the heavy cream in a stand mixer bowl. Fit the mixer with the whisk attachment and start it on a speed low enough to keep the cream from splashing out of the bowl.

2   Once the cream has formed soft peaks, turn the speed up to medium-high. As you continue to whip, the cream will go past the stiff-peaks stage and the buttermilk will start to separate. As soon as this happens, stop the mixer, and wrap plastic wrap over the top of the mixer and sides of the bowl to contain splashes *(Photo A, page 137)*.

3   Turn the mixer to medium-low speed and whip until there's quite a bit of liquid and pebbles of butter begin to form *(Photo B, page 137). Continued ›*

The following flavour variations assume a yield of about 375 g of finished butter. The quantities are flexible. Feel free to adjust up and down as you see fit.

CRANBERRY ORANGE

zest of 1 orange
⅓ cup finely chopped dried cranberries
reduce the fleur de sel (sea salt) to ⅛ tsp

GARLIC HERB

1 garlic clove, finely chopped
2 tsp finely chopped fresh parsley
2 tsp finely chopped fresh thyme
2 tsp finely chopped fresh chives
¼ tsp ground black pepper

HONEY ROSEMARY

80 g (¼ cup) honey
1 Tbsp finely chopped fresh rosemary
reduce the fleur de sel (sea salt) to ⅛ tsp

4   Place a fine-mesh sieve over a large bowl. Pour in the contents of the mixer bowl and shake around to drain out the buttermilk, taking care not to push the butter through the sieve *(Photo C)*. Pour the buttermilk into a container and chill it to use later for another purpose. Shape the butter into a ball with your hands.

5   Prepare a bowl with very cold water and place the butter in it. Massage it around with your hands *(Photo D)*. The water will become cloudy. Drain the butter again (discarding the murky water) and repeat the process with fresh cold water until the water is completely clear after massaging, usually 3 or 4 washes. The butter is now ready to be flavoured.

6   Place the butter back into the stand mixer bowl. Add the salt and any flavour additions and, using the paddle attachment, mix until well blended, about 1 minute.

7   If you are using a wooden butter mould, soak the mould in ice water for about 10 minutes prior to using. Fill the mould with butter, scraping off the top to give it a smooth edge, and then knock the butter out onto a piece of parchment paper. If you are going to wrap the shaped butter to give away as gifts, freeze the unmoulded butter before wrapping.

If you are not using a mould, roughly shape the butter into a log with your hands. Place it on a piece of plastic wrap. Fold the wrap over the log and, using a ruler or a flat bench scraper, push the butter firmly to one side. Twist the ends of the plastic wrap and roll the log back and forth to even out the shape *(Photo E)*. Freeze for 20 minutes before slicing into rounds *(Photo F)*.

STORAGE

Homemade butter will keep for up to two weeks in the refrigerator or for up to six months in the freezer.

SOUPE À L'OIGNON
French Onion Soup

Serves 8—

BEEF STOCK

2–2.5 kg (about 5 lb) beef bones
3 medium carrots
2 celery ribs
1 leek, cleaned, white part only
1 large onion
2 garlic cloves
75 g (¼ cup) tomato paste
4 L (16 cups) water
1 bay leaf

SOUP

4 onions, thinly sliced (about 5 cups)
1 garlic clove, finely diced
1 Tbsp unsalted butter
240 g (1 cup) red wine
2 L (8 cups) beef stock
2 sprigs fresh thyme
2 tsp salt
1 tsp ground black pepper

TOPPING

4 cups cubed day-old bread
3 Tbsp olive oil
salt and ground black pepper
about 200 g (2 cups) grated gruyère
    cheese

INGREDIENT NOTES

For the croutons, I like to use sourdough
bread. Bones for roasting and making stock
are easily obtained from your local butcher.

EQUIPMENT

You will need eight ovenproof soup bowls and
a baking sheet.

We used to serve this French onion soup at the Bake Shop, and it was so popular that we were spending long hours roasting beef bones for stock and preparing vegetables. Unfortunately, the overwhelming smell of onions in our kitchen was affecting our pastries, so we had to take it off the menu. I do miss eating the soup at work, but I still enjoy making it at home, especially on a cold winter's day.

The key to a great French onion soup is a deep, dark stock with well-developed flavours. The homemade stock provided in this recipe fits the bill. Since it freezes well, you could even double or triple it for future soup-making. If you don't have time to make your own stock, you can replace it with a good-quality store-bought beef stock, but you will lose out on some of the flavour that roasted beef bones and vegetables provide to a homemade stock.

TO MAKE THE STOCK

1   Preheat your oven to 425°F (220°C).

2   Place the bones in a roasting pan and roast until dark brown, about 30 minutes (45 minutes if they are frozen). While the bones are roasting, chop the carrots, celery, leek, and onion into large pieces.

3   When the bones are dark brown, add the vegetables to the roasting pan, stir, and roast for another 45 minutes.

4   Add the garlic and tomato paste to the roasting pan and give everything a good stir. Roast for about another 20 minutes, until the tomato paste is dark brown and partially charred.

5   Transfer all the bones and vegetables to a large stock pot. Add some of the water to the roasting pan and scrape the bottom well to deglaze. Add this to the stock pot, along with the remaining water and bay leaf. Bring to a boil, and then simmer uncovered for 4 hours. Skim off any excess fat, strain the stock, and discard the solids. Set aside 8 cups and freeze the rest for future use. *Continued ›*

TO MAKE THE SOUP

6 Place the onions, garlic, and butter in a large sauce-pan. On medium-low heat, gently cook until the onions are dark brown and well caramelized. Stir every 5 to 10 minutes, making sure to scrape the bottom of the saucepan well each time. It can take up to 45 minutes for the onions to fully caramelize.

7 Once the onions are caramelized, add the red wine, scraping the bottom of the saucepan well. Continue to cook until the wine has reduced slightly.

8 Add the remaining soup ingredients and simmer for 1 hour. Adjust the salt and pepper as needed.

TO FINISH THE SOUP

9 To make the croutons, preheat your oven to 350°F (180°C). Toss the bread cubes, olive oil, salt, and pepper together and spread them out on a baking sheet. Bake for 10 to 15 minutes, until golden brown and crispy.

10 When ready to serve, set your oven to broil. Ladle the hot soup into ovenproof soup bowls. Top each serving with a handful of croutons and grated gruyère. Place under the broiler until the cheese is bubbling and brown. Serve hot.

STORAGE

This soup will keep in the refrigerator for up to one week and can be frozen for up to six months.

Relaxing in the Loire valley.

Apple Leek Camembert
QUICHE

Makes one 9-inch deep-dish quiche —

INGREDIENTS

1 blind-baked pie shell (deep-dish)
  (page 80)
1 leek, cleaned, white part only, thinly
  sliced
1 Tbsp unsalted butter
110 g (½ cup) French cider *(see note)*
1 apple, peeled, cored, and sliced about
  ½ cm thick *(see tips, page 133)*
2 Tbsp all-purpose flour
1 tsp salt
½ tsp ground black pepper
3 large eggs
525 g (2¼ cups) whipping cream
120 g (½ cup) whole milk
125 g (1 cup) diced camembert or
  pont-l'évêque cheese, diced in 2-cm
  cubes

INGREDIENT NOTE

Be sure to use French cider in this recipe
for the best results; it is common in North
American liquor stores and quite affordable.
It tends to be a bit on the drier side and has a
particular taste profile different from North
American ciders.

EQUIPMENT

This recipe is designed for a 9-inch deep-
dish pie plate. If you're using a regular pie
plate, you may have some extra filling.

*The year before we had our first child, Benoît, Jacob and
I spent a magical two weeks in Normandy with some good
friends. We rented a little cottage and spent our days explor-
ing the countryside, drinking buckets of French cider, and
indulging in local specialties. This quiche, my tribute to this
memorable holiday, features all of my favourite Normandy
foods: apples, cider, soft cheese, and leeks.*

PROCEDURE

1   Preheat your oven to 375°F (190°C).

2   In a saucepan over medium-low heat, gently cook
    the leek in the butter until dark brown and well
    caramelized, stirring occasionally. This may take up
    to 10 minutes.

3   Once the leek is caramelized, add the cider, making
    sure to scrape the bottom of the saucepan well.
    Continue to cook until the majority of the cider has
    evaporated. Remove from heat, stir in the sliced
    apples, and set aside.

4   In a bowl, combine the flour, salt, and pepper. Add
    the eggs and whisk well, until most of the lumps
    have disappeared.

5   Add the whipping cream and milk and whisk until
    well combined. Pour the custard into the blind-baked
    pie shell, filling to three-quarters full. Sprinkle the
    leeks, apples, and cheese cubes over the custard.

6   Bake for 45 to 55 minutes, until the centre is just set
    (add 10 minutes if you're using a ceramic pie plate).
    If the outside of the crust starts to look dark during
    baking, cover the quiche with foil.

SERVING & STORAGE

This quiche is best served warm out of the oven. It will
keep in the refrigerator for up to three days. Briefly
reheat it in the oven before serving.

CROQUE-MONSIEURS

Makes 4 sandwiches —

MORNAY SAUCE

2 Tbsp unsalted butter
¼ cup finely diced shallots or yellow
    onion
1 clove garlic, finely chopped
2 Tbsp all-purpose flour
475 g (2 cups) whole milk
2 sprigs fresh thyme (¼ tsp dried)
½ tsp salt
½ tsp ground black pepper
50 g (½ cup) grated gruyère cheese
25 g (¼ cup) grated parmesan cheese
1 Tbsp creamy Dijon mustard

SANDWICHES

olive oil, for frying
8 slices good-quality sourdough bread
250–300 g (8–10 oz) smoked ham, thinly
    sliced
about 200 g (2 cups) gruyère cheese,
    grated

INGREDIENT NOTE

To turn your croque-monsieur into a
croque-madame, simply top with a fried egg.

*A baked ham and cheese sandwich with a rich white sauce?
Yes, please! A good croque-monsieur is almost a religious
experience. This can only be achieved by choosing your
ingredients with extra-special care. I use a sourdough
bread with a nice crust and chewy texture, ham that's been
smoked and cured from my local deli, and quality gruyère
cheese that has great flavour and melts beautifully.*

*The other key to a good croque-monsieur is a flavourful
sauce. I prefer mornay (a cheesy béchamel) for that added
decadence. Trying to calculate how many calories are in
a croque-monsieur will make your head spin, but it's so
sinfully delicious that it is well worth it!*

TO MAKE THE MORNAY SAUCE

1   In a saucepan over medium-low heat, melt the
    butter. Add the shallots and garlic and sauté until
    translucent and soft.

2   Sprinkle in the flour and continue to cook for
    2 minutes. Slowly drizzle in the milk, whisking
    constantly. If you add the milk too quickly, your
    sauce will end up lumpy. Once the milk has been
    fully incorporated, add the sprigs of thyme, salt,
    and pepper.

3   Reduce the heat to low and simmer for 15 to 20
    minutes, stirring occasionally, until the sauce has
    thickened. Pass through a fine-mesh sieve.

4   Return to low heat and add the gruyère, parme-
    san, and mustard. Stir until the cheese is melted.
    Continued ›

5   Preheat your oven to 375°F (180°C).

6   In a frying pan over medium heat, heat a few table-spoons of olive oil. Fry each slice of bread on each side until crispy, sprinkling with a bit of salt while frying. You may need to add more olive oil to the pan between slices.

7   Lay out 4 slices of fried bread on a baking sheet. Generously spread each slice with mornay sauce and top with a quarter of the ham and ¼ cup of gruyère.

8   Leaving the sandwiches open-face, place in the oven for 8 to 10 minutes, until the cheese has melted. Remove from the oven and set the oven to broil.

9   Add a second piece of bread over each sandwich. Generously spread the remaining mornay sauce all over the tops, including the crusts. Sprinkle with the remaining gruyère. Broil until the cheese is bubbling and the tops are golden brown. Serve immediately.

SERVING & STORAGE

Croque-monsieurs should be served as soon as they come out of the oven. The mornay sauce will keep, refrigerated and well covered, for up to four days.

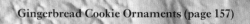

Gingerbread Cookie Ornaments (page 157)

Noël

CHRISTMAS

NOËL (CHRISTMAS) IS BY FAR the best food holiday of the year. For many families, traditions and memories are created in the kitchen as people gather with loved ones to celebrate with a meal. Being French-Canadian, the food that we will eat at réveillon (our Christmas Eve celebration) is the most talked-about thing all through December. From a young age, Christmas for me wasn't about the gifts I would get to open but rather the delicious food I would get to eat.

Now that we own our own bakery, our reality is that we don't often get to celebrate the way that we used to. Despite this, we still do our best to see as much family as we can and get in the kitchen with our children. I've taken many of my family's recipes and traditions and incorporated them into our holiday menu at the Bake Shop, and every year it warms my heart thinking about all of the families and friends that are gathered together enjoying the treats we lovingly made for them.

"IF MORE OF US VALUED FOOD AND CHEER AND SONG ABOVE HOARDED GOLD, IT WOULD BE A MERRIER WORLD."
—THORIN, *THE HOBBIT*

MINCEMEAT STARS

MINCEMEAT FILLING

1 large Granny Smith apple
65 g (½ cup) dates
55 g (⅓ cup) prunes
50 g (¼ cup) water
zest of 1 medium orange
2 Tbsp orange juice
zest of 1 lemon
1 Tbsp lemon juice
45 g (⅓ cup) dried currants
50 g (⅓ cup) Thompson raisins
40 g (⅓ cup) dried cranberries
40 g (¼ cup) sultana raisins
60 g (⅓ cup lightly packed) dark brown
    sugar
25 g (3 Tbsp) orange juice
¼ tsp ground ginger
⅛ tsp ground cloves
⅛ tsp ground cinnamon
2 Tbsp brandy *(optional)*

ASSEMBLY

1 batch Easy Mixer Pie Dough, cold
    (page 80)
1 large egg white
1 tsp milk or cream
sanding or decorating sugar *(optional)*

INGREDIENT NOTE

Don't be deterred by the mincemeat's long
list of ingredients. Visiting the bulk section of
your grocery store is a great way to buy only
exactly what you need. As this recipe makes
more mincemeat than you will need, you can
freeze the extra and use it at a later time, or
make another batch of pie dough to increase
the number of cookies.

EQUIPMENT

You will need two baking sheets and a 3- or
4-inch round cookie cutter.

*When I was growing up, one of my mother's annual
Christmas recipes was for rolled mincemeat cookies. I
remember the unappetizing jar of mincemeat in the cold
room that seemed to sit there for years. I would eat the
cookie around the edges and sneakily throw the mincemeat
centre away. As I grew older, I eventually graduated to
eating the whole cookie, and today, mincemeat—in all its
complexity—is one of my favourite holiday flavours.*

*Although traditional mincemeat is made with beef or
venison suet, I've created this modern-day version that's a
bit more in tune with my personal taste. Jam-packed with
an assortment of dried fruit, bold spices, and tangy citrus,
this update on the classic would surely have won over my five-
year-old self.*

TO MAKE THE MINCEMEAT FILLING

1   Peel, core, and finely dice the apple *(see tips, page 133)*.
    Roughly chop the dates and prunes into small
    pieces. In a saucepan, combine the water, dates,
    prunes, orange zest, first measure of orange juice,
    lemon zest, and lemon juice. Bring to a boil and
    simmer for 5 minutes, stirring occasionally.

2   Add the remaining ingredients (except the brandy)
    and, stirring occasionally, simmer on low for about
    10 minutes, until the fruit has softened and broken
    down. Remove from heat and stir in the brandy,
    if using. At this point, you may purée the mince-
    meat or leave it chunky—your preference. Cool
    completely.

TO ASSEMBLE THE COOKIES

3   Before rolling out your dough, preheat your oven to
    375°F (190°C). Line the baking sheets with parch-
    ment paper. Make sure your dough is fully chilled
    when you start working with it. The filling must also
    be completely cool. *Continued ›*

4   Lightly flour your work surface and place half of the cold dough in the middle, leaving the rest in the refrigerator. Lightly flour the top of the dough and, using a rolling pin, begin rolling the dough from the centre outward.

5   Keep rotating the dough as you roll it out, lightly flouring the surface under the dough as well as the top as needed to prevent it from sticking. Roll it out to about ½ cm thick.

6   Using a round cookie cutter, cut out 12 cookie bases and arrange them on a lined baking sheet *(Photo A)*. Place a heaping teaspoon of mincemeat filling in the centre of each *(Photo B)* and flatten slightly with the back of a spoon or your finger. Place the baking sheet in the refrigerator before you move on to the next step. It's important to keep your pie dough cold.

7   Roll out the second half of the pie dough, cutting out 12 cookie tops with the same round cutter. Gather up all your pie dough scraps, wrap them, and refrigerate.

8   Gently fold each circle in half and cut a line down the middle but not all the way to the edge. Open the circle, turn it, and fold it in half along the cut line. Cut a line down the middle, intersecting the fold, and then cut a diagonal line on each side, like a fan *(Photo C)*. Alternatively, feel free to use a decorative cutter to cut a vent hole.

9   Remove the tray of cookie bases from the refrigerator. Using your finger, dab a bit of water around the edges of a cookie base. Lay a scored circle overtop and press the edges down firmly, being careful not to push any of the filling out. Repeat for the remaining bases. *Continued ›*

10 Make egg wash by whisking together the cream and egg white. Brush it generously over the cook‑ies and sprinkle generously with sanding sugar. Bake for 25 to 30 minutes, until the tops are a light golden brown.

11 Once the scraps have rested in the refrigerator for about a half hour, re-roll, fill, and bake them as above. The dough will be a bit tougher, so a bit of elbow grease will be required. The dough can be re-rolled only once.

STORAGE

These cookies will keep at room temperature for up to five days and can be frozen for up to three months.

FEUILLANTINES

Makes 24 large cookies —

INGREDIENTS

470 g (3¼ cups) all-purpose flour

1¾ tsp baking soda

½ tsp salt

225 g (1 cup) unsalted butter, at room temperature

200 g (1 cup + 2 Tbsp firmly packed) golden brown sugar

2 large eggs, at room temperature

120 g (⅓ cup) light corn syrup

1 tsp vanilla extract or paste

about 1½ cups jelly, for filling

INGREDIENT NOTES

In order for your butter and eggs to cream properly, make sure they are at room temperature before starting. I fill the feuillantines with crabapple or apple jelly, but you can use any jam or jelly of your choosing.

EQUIPMENT

You will need two to four baking sheets and a stand mixer fitted with a paddle attachment. If you only have two baking sheets, while your first batch is baking, keep your scraps in the refrigerator.

This simple cookie recipe has been in my father's family for over a century. When my parents got married, my mother carried on the tradition of making them at Christmas for our family. My earliest memory of baking is of making these with her. I would help her cut out different cookie shapes and fill them warm out of the oven with jelly. She would then put them in a big tin and 'hide' them in our cold room, where I would sneak some whenever I got a chance.

On the day feuillantines are made, they are a bit crunchy, but they soon soften up—delicious both ways!

PROCEDURE

1 Preheat your oven to 350°F (180°C). Line the baking sheets with parchment paper.

2 Sift together the flour, baking soda, and salt. Set aside.

3 Place the butter and brown sugar in the bowl of a stand mixer. Cream on medium speed for 2 minutes, or until light and fluffy. Scrape down the sides of the bowl as needed.

4 Add the eggs, corn syrup, and vanilla and mix until well incorporated.

5 Turn the mixer down to low speed and add the flour mixture. Mix until just combined, scraping down the sides of the bowl as needed.

6 Divide the dough and shape it into 2 flat round circles, wrap them in plastic wrap, and refrigerate for at least 1 hour, until chilled. *Continued ›*

7   On a lightly floured surface, roll out the dough to about ½ cm thick. Using cookie cutters, cut out shapes and gently place about 2 inches apart on the baking sheets. Continue to re-roll dough scraps and cut shapes until all the dough has been used.

8   Bake for 12 to 14 minutes, until the cookies have darkened slightly.

9   While the cookies are still warm, sandwich pairs of cookies with a layer of jelly.

STORAGE

Feuillantines will keep at room temperature for up to five days or in the freezer for up to three months.

My mother, Sylvia, and me, making feuillantines with Rose and Benoît.

GINGERBREAD
Cookie Ornaments

Makes 24 large cookies —

INGREDIENTS

525 g (3⅔ cups) all-purpose flour

1 Tbsp cocoa powder

3 tsp ground ginger

2 tsp ground cinnamon

1½ tsp ground cloves

1 tsp salt

½ tsp baking soda

225 g (1 cup) unsalted butter, at room
    temperature

150 g (¾ cup) sugar

1 large egg, at room temperature

155 g (½ cup) fancy molasses

2 Tbsp white corn syrup

1 batch Royal Icing *(page 159)*

INGREDIENT NOTE

In order for your butter and egg to cream
properly, make sure they are at room
temperature before starting.

EQUIPMENT

You will need a stand mixer with a paddle
attachment, two or three baking sheets, and a
few small piping bags and decorating tips.

*These cookies are spicy and not too sweet, with the perfect
snap—and they make tempting edible ornaments for the
Christmas tree. Although they can be left plain, a fun
activity to do with children is to decorate them with royal
icing. They will also have fun playing with different
cookie shapes.*

TO MAKE THE COOKIES

1 Preheat your oven to 350°F (180°C). Line the
baking sheets with parchment paper.

2 Sift together all the dry ingredients and set aside.

3 Place the butter and sugar in the bowl of a stand
mixer. Cream on medium speed for 2 minutes,
scraping down the sides of the bowl as needed.

4 Add the egg, molasses, and corn syrup and mix for
1 minute. Scrape down the sides of the bowl.

5 Turn the mixer down to low speed. Add the sifted
dry ingredients and mix until the dough starts to
come together. Stop the mixer, scrape down the
bowl, and mix again until the dough fully comes
together. The dough will be fairly soft.

6 Shape the dough into a flat round circle, wrap with
plastic wrap, and refrigerate for 15 to 20 minutes,
until it is set enough to roll out without falling
apart. At this point the dough can be kept chilled
for up to 2 days or frozen for up to 6 months.

7 On a lightly floured surface, roll out the dough to
½ cm thick. *Continued ›*

8 Using a cookie cutter, cut out shapes and gently place them about 2 inches apart on the baking sheets. Continue to re-roll dough scraps and cut shapes until all the dough has been used. If you're planning on making ornaments to hang, use a small round shape (such as the end of a piping tip or straw) to make a hole in the desired spot on the cookie.

Note: If you are working in a warm kitchen or your cookie dough got quite warm while being rolled out, chill your baking sheets in the freezer or refrigerator for 5 to 10 minutes before baking. This will prevent the cookies from spreading during baking.

9 Bake for 13 to 15 minutes, until the cookies have darkened slightly.

TO DECORATE THE COOKIES

Use Royal Icing *(facing page)* to decorate the ginger-bread cookies. I like to use small piping bags and tips to get nice smooth lines of icing. If you don't have those, it's fine to use a spoon or a knife to spread the icing around. Have fun playing with different colours of icing and patterns. Make sure the icing is completely dry before threading a ribbon through the hole.

STORAGE

These cookies will keep at room temperature for up to a week. If using for ornaments, they will technically be edible after an extended period of time, though probably stale and a bit dusty!

ROYAL ICING

Makes about 2 cups—

INGREDIENTS
360 g (3 cups) icing sugar
4 tsp egg albumen (or meringue powder)
¼ tsp cream of tartar
80 g (⅓ cup) water, at room temperature
½ tsp vanilla extract or paste
gel food colouring *(optional)*

INGREDIENT NOTES
The egg albumen is key to this icing's stability. If you don't have egg albumen, meringue powder will also do the trick. If using water-based liquid food colouring, you may need to add less water in step 3.

EQUIPMENT
You will need a stand mixer with a whisk attachment.

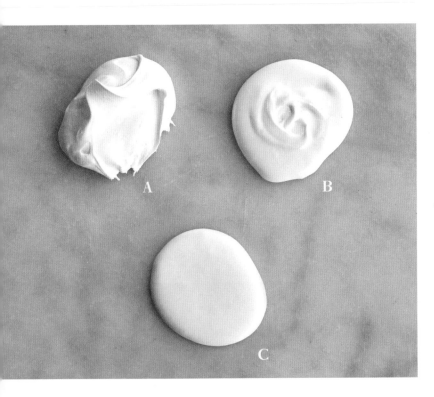

This is a trusty and versatile icing that will never let you down. It can be used as glue for a gingerbread house, as fondant dip, or to flood and decorate cookies. The recipe is courtesy of my good friend Amanda.

PROCEDURE

1   Sift together the icing sugar, egg albumen, and cream of tartar into the bowl of a stand mixer. Add the water and mix on low speed until smooth.

2   Scrape down the sides of the bowl and add the vanilla extract. Beat the icing on medium speed for about 5 minutes, until stiff peaks form. The icing will be quite thick. Remove the bowl from the mixer.

3   Next, you may need to add more water to the icing depending on the specific purpose:

   - **As 'glue' for a gingerbread house—**
     Use stiff right out of the bowl *(Photo A)*.
   - **For decorating Gingerbread Cookie Ornaments** *(page 157)—*
     Add 1 Tbsp water and mix it in using a spatula. The icing should be pipeable but still hold a bit of a shape *(Photo B)*. If it still seems too stiff, add another teaspoon of water and mix again. Repeat until you have the right consistency.
   - **To dip madeleines** *(page 164)—*
     Add 1 to 2 Tbsp water and mix it in using a spatula. It should be quite soft and not hold much of a shape *(Photo C)*.

4   Once the desired texture is achieved, divide the icing and colour with the colours of your choice. Immediately store in well-sealed containers until ready to use. Royal icing will dry out quickly if exposed to air.

STORAGE
Royal icing will keep well sealed in the refrigerator for up to a week.

Gingerbread
PINWHEEL

Makes one 8-inch pinwheel—

GINGERBREAD SHORTBREAD

200 g (1⅓ cups) all-purpose flour
¾ tsp ground ginger
¼ tsp ground cinnamon
⅛ tsp ground cloves
⅛ tsp ground allspice
½ tsp salt
145 g (⅔ cup) unsalted butter, at room
  temperature
70 g (⅓ cup) dark brown sugar
40 g (2 Tbsp) fancy molasses
30 g (2 Tbsp) whole milk

ASSEMBLY

½ batch Mincemeat Filling *(page 149)*

GLAZE

60 g (½ cup) icing sugar
½ tsp egg albumen (or meringue powder)
pinch of cream of tartar
1 Tbsp water
a few drops vanilla extract or paste

INGREDIENT NOTE

If you have no other plans for your extra
half batch of mincemeat, a great option is to
double the gingerbread shortbread recipe and
make two pinwheels back to back.

EQUIPMENT

You will need a stand mixer fitted with a paddle
attachment. You will also need a ceramic
shortbread pan. Alternatively you can use a
non-ceramic shortbread pan or an 8-inch cake
pan, but the baking time will vary, so keep a
careful eye on the shortbread as it bakes.

*This is by far my favourite Christmas treat. I've been known
to eat the whole 8-inch cookie in one sitting! The spiced shortbread dough together with the homemade mincemeat is absolutely craveable, and I find it impossible to have only one piece.
The beautiful pattern on our ceramic shortbread pans gives it
a lovely decorative finish, and reminds me of the pinwheels
I would play with as a child. This cookie is perfect for cutting
into pieces for your holiday table or lovely as a hostess gift.*

TO MAKE THE GINGERBREAD SHORTBREAD

1 Sift together the flour, ginger, cinnamon, cloves,
   allspice, and salt. Set aside.

2 Place the butter and brown sugar in the bowl of a
   stand mixer. Cream on medium speed for 2 minutes,
   scraping down the sides of the bowl as needed.

3 Add the molasses and milk and mix until well incorporated. Scrape down the sides of the bowl. Add the
   dry ingredients and, with the mixer on low speed,
   mix until just incorporated.

4 Divide the dough into two equal parts and shape each
   portion into a flat circle. Wrap well in plastic wrap
   and let rest in the refrigerator for 20 to 30 minutes,
   until the dough has chilled enough to roll out.

TO ASSEMBLE THE PINWHEEL

5 Preheat your oven to 350°F (180°C). Generously
   spray the shortbread pan with vegetable oil.

6 Work with one circle of dough at a time. Lightly
   flour a work surface and both sides of the dough.
   Roll out the dough to about ¼ inch thick, checking
   often to ensure it's not sticking to your work surface.

7 Place the shortbread pan upside down on the rolled-
   out dough and gently press down to make an indent.
   Remove the pan and, using a knife, cut a circle out
   about 1 cm inside of the indentation so that you end
   up with a circle that is slightly smaller than the original
   (Photo A, page 162). *Continued ›*

8   Take the dough circle and, using your hands, firmly press it into the bottom of the shortbread pan, making sure to push it all the way to the edge *(Photo B)*.

9   Spread the mincemeat evenly over the dough, leaving about a ½ inch of room around the edges *(Photo C)*. Using your fingers, dab a bit of water around the edges.

10 For the top, repeat steps 6 and 7 with your second dough circle. Place the circle on top of the mincemeat. Gently press around the edges to seal, taking care to not push any of the filling out. Using a fork, dock the dough, making sure you push the fork all the way through *(Photo D)*.

11 Bake for 40 to 45 minutes, until the edges have browned. Let the pinwheel cool for about 10 minutes before unmoulding, and let cool completely before decorating.

TO MAKE THE GLAZE

12 Sift the icing sugar, egg albumen or meringue powder, and cream of tartar in a bowl.

13 Add the water and vanilla and, using a fork or a small whisk, mix until smooth. The icing should be just thin enough to spread but not runny.

14 Pour the icing onto the centre of the pinwheel. Using a pastry brush or knife, spread it outward towards the edge of the cookie, being careful not to get any down the sides. Run the pastry brush back and forth over the cookie to smooth out the icing, making sure to get it in all the nooks and scraping off any excess. The icing will dry in about 15 minutes.

SERVING & STORAGE

To serve the pinwheel, slice it into eight pieces. It will keep, well wrapped, for up to seven days at room temperature or for three months in the freezer.

Gingerbread
MADELEINE TREE

Makes 24 madeleines —

INGREDIENTS

160 g (1 cup + 2 Tbsp) all-purpose flour
½ tsp baking powder
4 large eggs, at room temperature
150 g (¾ cup firmly packed) dark brown
  sugar
150 g (⅔ cup) unsalted butter, melted and
  cooled
2 tsp vanilla extract or paste
1½ tsp ground ginger
½ tsp ground cinnamon
¼ tsp ground cloves

1 batch Royal Icing *(page 159)*
sprinkles, for decorating *(optional)*

EQUIPMENT

You will need a madeleine pan. These are
becoming easier to find in specialty kitchen
stores and online. It's hard to come up with
an alternative pan to use as it's the distinc-
tive shell shape that makes the madeleine
unique; however, a mini-muffin pan will also
do. If you need to bake the madeleines in
two batches, the pan needs to be washed and
cooled down for the second batch.

*These fun and festive little French tea cakes will be
snapped right up from your Christmas baking table.
Madeleine batter is quick and easy to prepare, bakes in no
time flat, and refrigerates and freezes really well, which
makes it quite versatile in the busy holiday period.*

*There are a wide variety of different madeleine baking
pans (silicone, nonstick, aluminum). Keep a sharp eye on
the baking time. It will vary from anywhere between 8 and
14 minutes depending on the type of pan you're using.*

PROCEDURE

1   Grease and flour the madeleine pan, tapping out any
    excess flour, and place it in the freezer or refrigera-
    tor so that it is cold when it comes time to fill it.

2   Mix the flour and baking powder in a small bowl
    and set aside.

3   Whisk together the eggs and sugar in a bowl until
    well combined. Add the butter, vanilla, and spices
    and whisk again.

4   Make a well in the centre of the dry ingredients,
    pour in the wet ingredients, and whisk until well
    combined. Cover with plastic wrap and refrigerate
    for at least 3 hours.

5   When ready to bake, preheat your oven to 400°F
    (200°C). Using a piping bag or a spoon, fill each
    madeleine cavity to just over three-quarters full.
    Bake for 10 to 12 minutes, until the madeleines are
    golden around the edges. You'll see a bump rise up
    in the middle of each madeleine—a sign of success!
    Continued ›

6   Once baked, immediately unmould the madeleines by gently tapping the pan over the counter. Set them aside to cool.

7   Dip the ruffled edge of each madeleine in the prepared royal icing. Use your finger to remove any excess icing or drips, and decorate with sprinkles if you like. Leave to dry completely before plating.

8   Once dry, arrange the madeleines in the shape of a tree on a decorative plate.

SERVING & STORAGE

Madeleines are best eaten the day they're baked, but dipping them in royal icing will extend their life a bit. The batter will keep for up to three days in the refrigerator or up to one month in the freezer.

GALETTE DES ROIS

Makes one 8-inch galette—

INGREDIENTS

1 package frozen puff pastry,
  enough to cut out two 8-inch circles
50 g (¼ cup) unsalted butter, at room
  temperature
50 g (¼ cup) sugar
50 g (½ cup) almond flour (finely ground
  almonds)
1½ tsp cornstarch
1 large egg
1½ tsp rum
½ tsp vanilla extract or paste
50 g (½ cup) sliced almonds
1 fève (a small ceramic tile or a large dry
  bean)
1 large egg yolk, beaten

ORANGE CHERRY VARIATION

Substitute the rum and the sliced almonds
with the zest of 1 orange or 2 Tbsp candied
orange peel and 50 g (⅓ cup) chopped
Amarena cherries.

INGREDIENT NOTE

If you are comfortable making your own puff
pastry, feel free to do so. A much faster option
is to buy pre-made frozen puff pastry. Make
sure you look for one that's all butter—it's
a bit pricier, but worth it for the quality and
flavour. See page 170 for tips on how to work
with puff pastry.

EQUIPMENT

You will need a baking sheet and a stand
mixer fitted with a paddle attachment.

*This traditional French galette is usually served around
January 6th to celebrate Epiphany, the arrival of the
Three Wise Men in Bethlehem. As a child, even though I
had no idea what Epiphany was, I looked forward to this
fun tradition every year.*

*To serve the galette, the youngest person in the room
hides under the table. Someone cuts the galette and serves
the pieces as the person under the table calls out which slice
goes to whom. The person lucky enough to find the fève
(bean) hidden inside is crowned king or queen and gets
to be the envy of all. In our house, it also meant that you
didn't have to help with the dinner dishes—a treat indeed!*

*The traditional filling is usually a plain crème d'aman-
des (almond cream), but in France, the leading pastry
chefs like to come up with their own unique flavours every
year. I've included one of my favourite variations.*

PREPARATION

1 Let the puff pastry defrost overnight in the refrigerator or on the counter for 15 to 20 minutes, making
   sure it's still cold when you come to work with it.

TO MAKE THE ALMOND CREAM

2 Place the butter and sugar in the bowl of a stand
   mixer. Cream on medium speed for about 2 minutes,
   until light and fluffy.

3 Add the almond flour and cornstarch and mix until
   well combined. Add the egg, rum, and vanilla. Mix
   for 2 minutes more, until smooth. Scrape down the
   sides of the bowl as needed.

4 Add the sliced almonds and mix until just combined.
   At this point, the almond cream can be refrigerated
   for up to 4 days—just make sure you re-whip it in the
   mixer before using it. *Continued ›*

TO ASSEMBLE AND BAKE THE GALETTE

5   Line the baking sheet with parchment paper and preheat your oven to 375°F (190°C). Make sure your almond cream is ready to go before you start working with the puff pastry.

6   Lightly flour your work surface and unroll or unfold your puff pastry. Lightly flour the top and, using a rolling pin, gently roll and smooth it out to get rid of any seams or bumps. Be careful not to roll it out too much or it will lose height during baking.

7   Using a plate or a saucepan lid as a guide, cut two 8-inch circles out of the puff pastry. Place one of the circles on your lined baking sheet. Lightly dock it all over with a fork *(Photo A)*.

8   Spread the almond cream over the puff-pastry base, doming it slightly in the centre and leaving about an inch around the edge. Hide the fève in the cream *(Photo B)*. Using your finger or a pastry brush, brush the edges with water.

9   Cut a small round vent hole in the centre of the second puff-pastry circle. Gently place the circle on top of the almond cream and seal the edges firmly. To flute the edge of the galette, use two fingers and the back of a knife to create a daisy edge *(Photo C)*.

10 Brush the top of the galette generously with the egg yolk, avoiding the sides. Refrigerate for 10 minutes, or until the yolk has set a bit.

11 Using a sharp knife, score lines in a fan outwards from the vent hole, expanding near the edge, being careful not to cut all the way through the dough *(Photo D)*. This will create a beautiful pattern on top when it bakes. Bake for 35 to 40 minutes, until the pastry is a deep golden brown. If at any point during baking the top puffs up dramatically in one area, poke it with a sharp knife to let steam escape. Let cool completely before serving.

SERVING & STORAGE

The galette is best served the day it's baked, but it will keep at room temperature for up to three days.

My father, André, crowned king.

Puff Pastry Tips & Tricks

- Be sure to buy good-quality frozen puff pastry made with real butter.
- Store puff pastry in the freezer. Only transfer it to the refrigerator if you plan on using it within five days.
- The most important thing to remember when working with puff pastry is to work with it cold. It also needs to be chilled before going in the oven, otherwise it will shrink.
- Generally, commercial puff pastry comes in a 10-inch square and rolled in a tube. To thaw it, pull it out of the package and let it thaw on the counter. This usually only takes 20 to 30 minutes (despite what the package often says!). Once thawed, gently unroll the tube. If you're not using it immediately, keep it in the refrigerator.
- If the puff pastry you buy comes rolled in a tube, it's always a good idea to roll it out a bit with a rolling pin to get it nice and flat before using it.

WHAT TO DO WITH YOUR PUFF PASTRY SCRAPS

When working with puff pastry there is no need to throw away trimmings. At the Bake Shop, we came up with a tasty way to use them up—Easy Puff Pastry Cheese Twists *(facing page)*. Making them takes very little time and can be done with very few scraps. You can use any variety of hard cheese you have in the house, which for me is usually a mixture of cheddar and gruyère. Parmesan is also great. If after making your main recipe you've run out of time, simply keep the scraps in a sealed bag in your refrigerator to make twists later (up to two days).

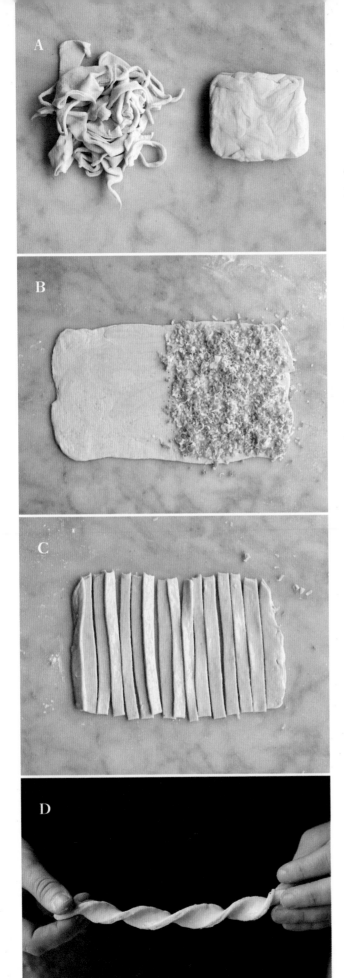

Easy Puff Pastry
CHEESE TWISTS

TO MAKE EASY CHEESE TWISTS

1   Smash the puff pastry scraps together into a ball, folding it over if you need to so that all the bits stick together. Roughly shape it into a square *(Photo A)*, flatten it a bit, and chill for 15 minutes. Preheat your oven to 375°F (190°C) and line a baking sheet with parchment paper.

2   Lightly flour a work surface and place the dough in the middle. Lightly flour the top and roll out into a roughly rectangular shape about 2 mm thick. As you roll, keep rotating the dough, lightly flouring the surface as needed so it doesn't stick.

3   Using a pastry brush or a damp, clean paper towel, lightly brush water over the whole surface of the dough, making sure not to dampen it too much.

4   Sprinkle grated cheese widthwise over half of the dough, followed by a bit of salt and pepper *(Photo B)*. Fold the dough over. Roll it out to flatten it, making sure the cheese is well stuck to the dough. Brush the top with egg yolk.

5   Using a sharp knife or a pizza wheel, cut the dough into 1½- to 2-cm strips *(Photo C)*. Pick up each strip and twist the ends in opposite directions *(Photo D)*. Place on the lined baking sheet about 2 inches apart and refrigerate for 15 minutes. Bake for 20 to 25 minutes, until light golden brown.

CINNAMON SUGAR VARIATION
Make the cheese twists above, simply replacing the cheese, salt, and pepper with a mixture of 4 parts sugar and 1 part cinnamon. Sprinkle a little additional sugar over the twists immediately before baking.

Makes 1 large bundt cake —

SALTED CHOCOLATE
¾ tsp fleur de sel (sea salt)
140 g (1 cup) milk or dark chocolate chunks

CAKE
255 g (1¾ cups) all-purpose flour
65 g (¼ cup) cocoa powder
1½ tsp baking powder
335 g (1½ cups) unsalted butter, at room
  temperature
315 g (1⅔ cups firmly packed) light
  brown sugar
6 large eggs
170 g (⅔ cup) mashed bananas (about
  2 small)
160 g (½ cup) orange marmalade
zest of 1 orange
100 g (¾ cup) crystallized ginger,
  chopped into small pieces

RUM SOAK
50 g (¼ cup) sugar
60 g (¼ cup) water
1 Tbsp rum
1 tsp fresh orange zest

CHOCOLATE GLAZE
225 g (1½ cups) milk or dark chocolate
  chunks
50 g (¼ cup) vegetable oil
crystallized ginger and cocoa nibs,
  for garnish

INGREDIENT NOTE
For the salted chocolate, it is very important to use fleur de sel (sea salt) rather than iodized table salt—its gentle flavour really enhances good-quality chocolate.

EQUIPMENT
You will need a 9- or 10-inch (10- or 15-cup) bundt pan, a baking sheet, a stand mixer fitted with a paddle attachment, a wire cooling rack, and an instant-read thermometer.

GÂTEAU D'HIVER
Winter Bundt Cake

Moist, chocolatey, and decadent, this cake is similar to a pound cake. I love the pops of salted chocolate throughout the cake, and the crystallized ginger and rum make a great combination. This cake is also equally good using dried or candied fruit instead of ginger.

Covering the cake in a chocolate glaze not only makes it more tasty, it also keeps it moist for longer. To not waste any chocolate, after the cake is glazed, I like to scrape the leftover chocolate off the tray, spread it onto a piece of parchment paper, and let it harden. I keep it in a container in my baking cupboard to re-melt and pour over ice cream or for dipping cookies.

TO MAKE THE SALTED CHOCOLATE

1 Line a baking sheet with parchment paper. If your fleur de sel is in big chunks, gently crush it up.

2 Slowly melt the chocolate over a double boiler or in a microwave on half power. Once melted, fold in the fleur de sel. Spread the chocolate out onto the parchment paper and place in the refrigerator *(Photo A, page 174)*. Once cold and set, crush it up into small pieces and set aside *(Photo B, page 174)*.

TO MAKE THE CAKE

3 Preheat your oven to 375°F (190°C). Butter and flour the bundt pan, tapping out any excess flour.

4 Sift together the flour, cocoa powder, and baking powder. Set aside.

5 Place the butter and brown sugar in the bowl of a stand mixer. Using a paddle attachment, cream on medium speed for about 2 minutes, until light and fluffy. Scrape down the sides of the bowl as needed.

6 Add the eggs one at a time, mixing until well incorporated. Turn the mixer down to low speed and add the flour mixture. Mix until just combined, scraping down the sides of the bowl as needed. *Continued ›*

7 Add the banana, orange marmalade, orange zest, and crystallized ginger. Mix until just combined. Remove the bowl from the mixer and gently fold in the crushed salted chocolate by hand.

8 Pour the batter into the prepared bundt pan. Bake for 15 minutes. Turn the heat down to 350°F (180°C) and bake for an additional 35 to 40 minutes, until the cake bounces back to the touch. Let the cake cool for 15 minutes before unmoulding it onto a cooling rack.

TO MAKE THE RUM SOAK

9 While the cake is baking, place the sugar and water in a small saucepan and heat until the syrup just comes to a boil. Remove from heat and stir in the rum and orange zest.

10 As soon as you've unmoulded the cake, using a pastry brush, generously brush it all over with the rum soak. Allow the cake to cool completely.

TO MAKE THE CHOCOLATE GLAZE & FINISH THE CAKE

11 Place the cooling rack with the cake on it over a baking tray to catch chocolate drips. Set aside.

12 Over a double boiler, melt the chocolate. Once completely melted, mix in the vegetable oil and let cool until it reaches a temperature of 40°C (105°F).

13 Using a large ladle or measuring cup, pour the glaze slowly over the top of the cake *(Photo C)*, making sure to cover all the sides. If you miss any spots, use a knife or your finger to cover them. Sprinkle crystallized ginger and cocoa nibs over the cake to garnish. Refrigerate until the glaze is set and transfer to a serving plate.

STORAGE

This cake will keep, well wrapped at room temperature, for up to five days.

Eggnog Chouquette Wreath (next page)

Serves 10—

PÂTE À CHOUX & ASSEMBLY

1 batch Pâte à Choux *(page 66)*, just
   made
1 large egg yolk, beaten
pearl sugar, for garnish

EGGNOG WHIPPED GANACHE

160 g (1¼ cups) white chocolate chunks
270 g (1¼ cups) whipping cream
⅛ tsp ground cloves
⅛ tsp ground nutmeg
⅛ tsp ground cinnamon
110 g (½ cup) whipping cream, cold
1 Tbsp rum

DARK CHOCOLATE GANACHE

70 g (½ cup) dark chocolate chunks
75 g (⅓ cup) whipping cream
1 Tbsp white corn syrup

INGREDIENT NOTES

Popular in Europe, pearl sugar, sometimes
referred to as nib sugar, is a hard sugar that
doesn't melt well at standard oven temperatures. Pearl sugar can be a bit tricky to find
in stores in North America but can easily
be obtained online. If you don't have pearl
sugar, you can use sliced almonds or cocoa
nibs instead.

For the white chocolate in the eggnog
whipped ganache recipe, I use Valrhona white
chocolate callets.

EQUIPMENT

You will need a stand mixer fitted with a
paddle attachment, a baking sheet, two
piping bags, and a large round piping tip
(#808 or #809).

*This lovely Christmas wreath is so fun to serve around
the holidays. Not only is it made of pâte à choux, one of
my favourite doughs, it also features whipped ganache, an
excellent base recipe I often use in desserts. The whipped
cream gives the ganache lightness, and the white chocolate
adds stability and makes it easy to pipe. I love the combination of eggnog and dark chocolate, but feel free to change
the flavour of the whipped ganache to your taste (pepper-
mint, gingerbread, cranberry...).*

*This recipe may seem like a lot of steps, but almost
everything can be made in advance. The exception is the
pâte à choux, which must be piped as soon as it is made.
The eggnog whipped ganache needs to sit in the refrigerator
for at least four hours or overnight for the chocolate to
crystallize and whip up properly.*

TO PIPE AND BAKE THE PÂTE À CHOUX

1   Preheat your oven to 375°F (190°C). Take a piece of
    parchment paper and trace the template for chou-
    quettes given on page 187. Flip the template over
    onto the baking sheet so that the lines are face down.

2   As soon as your pâte à choux is made, use a small
    amount to glue down the corners of the template
    to the baking sheet. This will prevent the template
    from slipping around while you're piping your
    chouquettes.

3   Fit a piping bag with a large round tip (#808 or
    #809). Fill the bag with the pâte à choux.

4   Position your piping tip a few centimetres above
    the template over the centre of a circle. Pipe
    out dough until it reaches the edge of the circle.
    Moving around clockwise, pipe the remaining
    circles *(Photo A, page 178)*. The dough circles will
    be touching. If you have any dough left after filling
    all the circles, pipe a few extra chouquettes similar
    in size in the corners of the parchment paper.
    Continued ›

5 Use your finger to gently run egg yolk over the top of each chouquette, smoothing down any bumps as you go. Sprinkle the chouquettes generously with pearl sugar *(Photo B)*.

6 Immediately bake the chouquettes for 30 minutes. Do not open the oven door during baking. After 30 minutes, open the oven door for 5 to 10 seconds to let the built-up steam escape and slightly dry out the dough. Bake for about another 8 to 10 minutes, until you can feel that the outside of the dough has crisped up. It should be a dark golden brown in colour *(Photo C)*.

7 Once baked, the choux ring should be filled and served over the next two days. If you didn't fill it right away and the choux has gone soft, re-crisp it in the oven for 4 to 6 minutes at 350°F (180°C). The baked ring can also be frozen for up to 2 months: in that case, place it frozen in a 350°F (180°C) oven until warmed through and crispy (6 to 8 minutes).

TO MAKE THE EGGNOG WHIPPED GANACHE
8 Slowly melt the white chocolate over a double boiler or on half power in a microwave. In a saucepan, heat the first measure of whipping cream and the spices until scalding (just before boiling).

9 Pour the hot cream over the chocolate in three parts, mixing vigorously with a spatula between each addition until smooth. Slowly whisk in the second measure of cream (cold) and rum. The mixture will be liquid.

10 Let the ganache set in the refrigerator at least 4 hours or overnight. It will have thickened slightly but still be quite liquid. *Continued ›*

TO MAKE THE DARK CHOCOLATE GANACHE

11 Slowly melt the dark chocolate over a double boiler or on half power in a microwave. In a small saucepan, heat the whipping cream and corn syrup until scalding.

12 Pour the hot cream over the melted chocolate in three parts, mixing vigorously with a spatula between each addition until smooth. Refrigerate for about 2 hours, until set.

TO ASSEMBLE THE WREATH

13 Make sure the choux ring is completely cool before proceeding. Using a serrated knife, gently cut the ring in half horizontally. If any of the chouquettes break apart, don't worry about it: once the ring is filled, it's easy to nicely set them back into place. Place the bottom half of the ring on a serving dish or platter.

14 Gently warm the dark chocolate ganache in the microwave for 10 to 20 seconds to soften it up. Spread it in a thin layer over the bottom of the shell, leaving about ½ inch of room around the edge. I find it easiest to use a piping bag with the tip cut off.

15 Using a stand mixer fitted with a paddle attachment, whip up the eggnog ganache until soft peaks form. Keep a close eye on it—if it overwhips it will start to separate and end up grainy.

16 Fit a piping bag with a large plain round tip and fill it with eggnog whipped ganache. Pipe a large dollop of ganache onto the bottom of each chouquette *(Photo D)*. Position the other half of the ring on top and press down gently.

SERVING & STORAGE

This eggnog wreath is best eaten the day it's made. If you're not serving it right away, keep it in the refrigerator for up to two days.

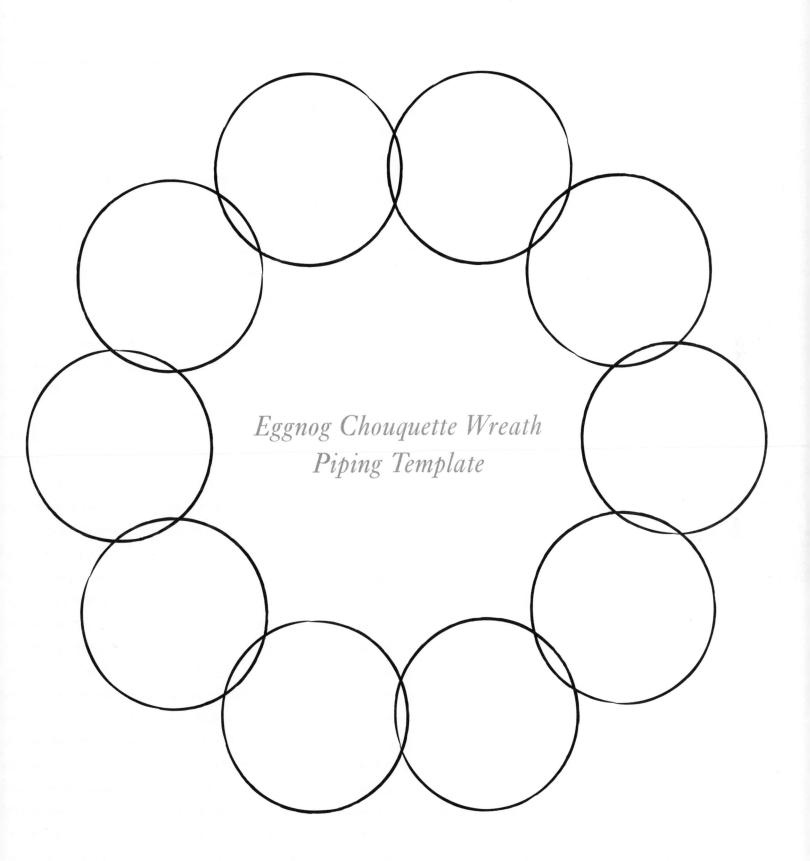

Eggnog Chouquette Wreath
Piping Template

Turkey Dinner
CHOUX

Serves 6—

INGREDIENTS

1 batch Pâte à Choux *(page 66),* **just made**

1 large egg yolk, beaten

turkey dinner leftovers, with all the fixings (don't forget the gravy!)

EQUIPMENT

You will need a stand mixer fitted with a paddle attachment (for the pâte à choux), a baking sheet, and a piping bag fitted with a large round piping tip (#807 or #809).

My favourite meal by far is turkey dinner. It's not just the turkey—it's all the fixings that go along with it too! As a turkey dinner traditionalist, I always keep strict control on our family turkey dinners. My mother is a very experimental cook and I'm always scared she'll decide to get creative and change something.

Sadly, because my birthday is in July, it's always too hot to make my favourite meal. But a few years ago, Jacob, knowing how much I like both pâte à choux (choux pastry) and turkey dinner, decided to surprise me. He piped and baked large choux buns, cut them open, and filled them with turkey dinner (including all the fixings!). It still amazes me that he slaved away in a hot kitchen in the middle of summer to make these. Needless to say, it was not only the best birthday ever, it was one of the tastiest things I've ever eaten.

Of course, the best time to make these is after Thanksgiving and Christmas when you have all of your turkey dinner leftovers. I try to make the choux buns in advance and have them in my freezer ready to go.

PROCEDURE

1   Preheat your oven to 375°F (190°C). Line a baking sheet with parchment paper.

2   Make your pâte à choux and immediately transfer it to a large piping bag fitted with a large round tip. Using a small amount of dough, glue down the corners of the parchment paper to the baking sheet to prevent it from slipping around as you pipe the buns.

3   Hold the piping bag vertically with the tip about 1 inch above the tray and pipe large circles, about 3 inches in diameter. Try to keep a steady hand so that the dough falls continuously in the centre of the circle. *Continued ›*

4 Use your finger to gently run egg yolk over the top of each circle, making sure to smooth down any bumps.

5 Bake immediately for 35 minutes. Do not open the oven door during baking. After 35 minutes, open the oven door for 5 to 10 seconds to let the built-up steam escape and slightly dry out the dough. Bake for another 5 to 10 minutes, until you can feel that the outside of the dough has crisped up. It should be a dark golden brown in colour.

6 Once the choux buns have cooled, using a serrated knife, cut each in half horizontally. Lift the top, fill with hot turkey dinner, and top with gravy. Serve immediately.

STORAGE

The baked buns will keep for three days at room temperature or three months in the freezer. When you're ready to use them, re-crisp them in the oven at 350°F (180°C) for 8 to 10 minutes.

SUGARPLUMS

This is my great-aunt's recipe, and these bite-sized balls are nothing like a conventional sugarplum. While her recipe called for Jell-O® powder, I've updated it to use fruit powder instead. These eye-catching little treats will liven up your cookie plate, and they're a big hit with kids!

Makes 25 sugarplums—

VANILLA CRUMBS

100 g (1 cup) cake flour
65 g (⅓ cup) sugar
pinch of salt
55 g (¼ cup) unsalted butter, at room temperature
½ tsp vanilla extract or paste

SUGARPLUMS

300 ml (1 can) sweetened condensed milk
40 g (⅓ cup) strawberry fruit powder
65 g (⅓ cup) sugar
150 g (1½ cups) unsweetened shredded coconut

FINISHING

1 tsp strawberry fruit powder
50 g (¼ cup) sugar
25 whole cloves

INGREDIENT NOTE

Fruit powder is fruit that has been freeze-dried and very finely ground. Fruit powder lends a lovely, intense flavour, but it can be a bit pricey. If you can't find it, strawberry Jell-O® powder will do.

EQUIPMENT

You will need a baking sheet and a food processor or coffee grinder.

TO MAKE THE VANILLA CRUMBS

1 Preheat your oven to 350°F (180°C) and line a baking sheet with parchment paper.

2 In a bowl, combine the flour, sugar, and salt. Add the butter and vanilla and, using your hands, work it into the dry ingredients until it starts to come together. It will look a bit dry.

3 Spread the mixture out on a baking sheet, clumping some of it with your fingers. Bake for 10 to 12 minutes, until a golden brown. Once cooled, pulse in a food processor or coffee grinder until it's broken down into fine crumbs.

TO MAKE THE SUGARPLUMS

4 Measure 1 cup of the vanilla crumbs into a bowl. Add the sweetened condensed milk, strawberry powder, sugar, and coconut and combine well. Any leftover crumbs can be kept covered at room temperature for another use, such as topping cupcakes or ice cream.

5 Make dusting powder by mixing the strawberry powder and sugar together in a bowl.

6 Form the dough into 1-inch balls and roll them in the dusting powder. My hands usually get pretty sticky halfway through so I wash and dry them before forming the other half of the dough. Press a whole clove into the top of each ball.

STORAGE

Sugarplums will keep for up to one week at room temperature. If you want to freeze them, do so before rolling them in the dusting powder and only dust them after you've let them thaw out.

Cardamom Orange
SABLÉS BRETONS

Makes 16 cookies —

SABLÉ BRETON DOUGH
180 g (1½ cups) cake flour
2 tsp baking powder
1 tsp ground cardamom
½ tsp salt
3 large egg yolks
120 g (⅔ cup) sugar
1 tsp vanilla extract or paste
130 g (½ cup + 2 Tbsp) unsalted butter,
    cubed, at room temperature
zest of 1 orange

FINISHING
1 large egg yolk, beaten
sanding sugar, or granulated sugar

INGREDIENT NOTES
For this recipe it's important that your butter
be at room temperature before starting.
    Sanding sugar is a shiny, coloured crystal
sugar that doesn't melt in the oven. It can
be easily purchased in a craft store or a bulk
foods store.

EQUIPMENT
You will need a 9-inch square baking pan and
a stand mixer fitted with a paddle attachment.

*These traditional French butter cookies are a snap to make.
They positively melt in your mouth and make a great
addition to any holiday cookie lineup. When they come out
of the oven they're soft and cakelike, changing to a lovely
flaky texture once cooled. The cardamom and orange
combination is perfect for the holidays, but if you aren't
a fan, simply omit those ingredients for a delicious plain
butter cookie. I have also provided you with suggestions for
alternative flavours at the end of the recipe.*

PROCEDURE

1 Butter a 9-inch square baking pan. In a bowl, sift
   the cake flour, baking powder, cardamom, and salt
   together and set aside.

2 Using a stand mixer fitted with a paddle attachment,
   whip the egg yolks and sugar on medium speed for
   about 2 minutes, until thickened and lightened in
   colour. Add the vanilla and mix until incorporated.

3 Add the sifted ingredients, butter, and orange zest.
   Mix until just incorporated.

4 Transfer the dough to the baking pan and press
   down with your hands *(Photo A, page 186)*, working
   it into all the corners. You may need to sprinkle a
   little flour on top so it doesn't stick to your fingers
   too much. Using something flat (such as a bowl
   scraper or an offset spatula), flatten the dough as
   best you can to make it even *(Photo B, page 186)*.
   Refrigerate for 1 hour.

5 Preheat your oven to 350°F (180°C). Brush the
   dough with an egg yolk and run a fork across it
   horizontally and vertically to create a criss-cross
   pattern *(Photo C, page 186)*. Sprinkle generously
   with sanding sugar. Bake for 25 to 30 minutes, until
   golden brown. *Continued ›*

6   While still warm, gently run a knife around the
    sides of the pan. Flip out the baked sablé and place
    it face up on a cutting board. Cut it into 16 square
    cookies, 3 cuts in each direction *(Photo D)*.

STORAGE

Sablés bretons will keep at room temperature for up to
one week.

*These cookies lend themselves so well to different
flavours. Here are a few suggestions to get you started,
but feel free to come up with your own! For the following
variations, omit the cardamom and orange zest—*

LEMON POPPYSEED

Add 3 tsp poppyseeds and the zest of 1 lemon.

CHOCOLATE PECAN

Add 60 g (⅓ cup) chocolate chunks, finely chopped,
and 30 g (¼ cup) pecans, finely chopped.

ROSEMARY

Add 3 tsp finely chopped rosemary.

TOASTED ALMOND

Add 60 g (½ cup) toasted slivered almonds, finely
chopped, and ¼ tsp almond extract.

MULLED
WINE & CIDER

MULLING SPICES
3 cinnamon sticks, plus extra for serving
3 whole star anise
¼ tsp black peppercorns
50 g (¼ cup) sugar (omit for the cider)
2 small chunks peeled fresh ginger
peel from 1 lemon
1 orange, thinly sliced

FOR MULLED CIDER
3 L (12 cups) apple juice

FOR MULLED WINE
750 ml (1 bottle) red wine
1 L (4 cups) apple juice

INGREDIENT NOTE
Using fresh spices will ensure that your mulled wine or cider comes out very flavourful and aromatic.

I love to have a pot of mulled wine or cider on the stove when I have guests over during the holidays. The apple cider option is great for kids, and a nice mug of warm mulled wine will be well appreciated by the adults on a chilly winter's day.

PROCEDURE
1   Place all the ingredients in a saucepan and simmer for about 30 minutes.

2   Serve hot. Add a cinnamon stick or orange slices to the mugs before serving.

SERVING
Mulled wine and mulled cider are best enjoyed the day they are made.

Croquembouche (page 223)

Occasions spéciales
CELEBRATIONS

Sometimes a celebration calls for an extra-special dessert—and sometimes I'm simply in the mood to make something more intricate. This chapter has some of my all-time favourite recipes for something a bit more sophisticated. Some of them have several parts, but don't let that put you off—in many cases they can be made ahead of time, which relieves some of the stress on celebration day. It just means a bit of planning. So go ahead—try that new ingredient, take on that challenge, and reap the rewards!

"AFTER A GOOD DINNER ONE CAN FORGIVE ANY-
BODY, EVEN ONE'S OWN RELATIVES."
—OSCAR WILDE

GÂTEAU SOLEIL
Sunshine Cake

Serves 8—

CAKE

250 g (2 cups + 1 Tbsp) cake flour
2½ tsp baking powder
3 large eggs
275 g (1⅓ cups) sugar
180 g (¾ cup) whole milk
150 g (⅔ cup) cold-pressed canola oil
   or olive oil

Ingredients continued ›

INGREDIENT NOTE

If you can't find cold-pressed canola oil, a
good-quality, fruity olive oil makes a great
substitute. Regular canola oil will also work.

EQUIPMENT

You will need a stand mixer fitted with a
paddle attachment, two 8-inch cake pans,
and a piping bag (or a resealable freezer bag).
A cake turntable is useful for finishing the
cake, but not necessary.

One of my favourite of Jacob's creations was a cake he
came up with for a pastry competition that he called
champ de soleil (field of sunshine). It starred citrus in
several forms, including the more obscure finger lime and
black lime, and cold-pressed canola oil. That cake was too
complex to recreate in a home kitchen, so I came up with
this adaptation aiming to capture as many of its flavours as
I could. The canola oil's deep yellow colour and nutty taste
work really well with the citrus and yogurt, and the dessert
is not too sweet.

I've never been great at cake decorating, so I keep the
finish on this cake pretty simple. If you've got cake decorating experience or are a piping wizard, by all means let
your creativity loose!

TO MAKE THE CAKE

1   Preheat your oven to 400°F (200°C). Spray the pans
with vegetable oil and line the bottoms with parchment
paper.

2   Sift the cake flour and baking powder together.
Set aside.

3   Using a stand mixer fitted with a paddle attachment,
mix the eggs and sugar on medium speed for 3 or 4
minutes, until light and fluffy. The mixture will be
almost white in colour.

4   Turn the mixer down to low speed and slowly drizzle
in the milk. Turn the mixer off and add the sifted
dry ingredients. Mix on low until just incorporated.
Scrape down the sides of the bowl.

5   Still on low speed, slowly drizzle in the oil and mix
until incorporated. Remove the bowl from the mixer
and give the batter a few more turns with your spatula,
making sure that everything is well incorporated
and there's nothing left in the bottom of the bowl.
Continued ›

CITRUS CURD

zest of 1 lemon
zest of 1 lime
115 g (½ cup + 1 Tbsp) sugar
2 large eggs
85 g (⅓ cup) mixture of freshly squeezed
   lemon and lime juice
150 g (⅔ cup) unsalted butter, at room
   temperature, cubed
1 whole lime

YOGURT CREAM

30 g (2 Tbsp) water, ice cold
6 g (2 tsp) powdered gelatin
180 g (¾ cup) whipping cream
1 Tbsp white corn syrup
245 g (1¾ cups) white chocolate chunks
180 g (¾ cup) plain yogurt (must be
   full-fat)
180 g (¾ cup) whipping cream, cold
⅛ tsp grated black lime *(optional)*

ASSEMBLY

mixed lemon and lime zest
grated black lime *(optional)*
fresh edible flowers *(optional)*

INGREDIENT NOTES

For the citrus juice, you can use a mixture of
lemon and lime. Orange and grapefruit juice
also work well in the mix.

Black lime (loomi)—lime that has been
brined and dried, popular in Middle Eastern
cooking—packs an amazing and unique
flavour punch in citrus desserts. You can purchase it in spice stores and specialty stores,
and it keeps indefinitely in your cupboard.
Go easy with it, as a little bit grated will go a
long way. If you can't find it, simply omit it
from this recipe.

The citrus curd and the yogurt cream
both need to chill for at least four hours
before assembly.

6   Divide the batter between the prepared pans. Bake
for about 25 minutes, until the cakes just spring
back to the touch. Once cooled enough to handle,
gently run a knife around the edge of each pan
and flip the cakes out onto a cooling rack to cool
completely.

Note: Over time I have learned that using 'fresh'
cake (just cooled out of the oven) makes cake assembly trickier than it needs to be. Instead, once your
cakes have cooled completely, place them in the
freezer for an hour before assembling. Your cakes
won't be as soft and will be much easier to work
with. If they have frozen rock hard, let them thaw
for 15 minutes before you work with them. The
cakes will keep wrapped in plastic in the freezer for
up to 3 months.

TO MAKE THE CITRUS CURD

7   In a bowl, rub the lemon and lime zest into the
sugar using your fingers to bring out the oils. Add
the eggs and whisk until well combined. Add the
citrus juice and whisk again.

8   Transfer to a double boiler. Cook over low heat for
25 minutes. The mixture will lose about half its
volume. It's important to whisk frequently, especially when the water really starts to boil, to avoid
the eggs scrambling and leaving you with a curd
that has an unpleasant texture. If you do see a few
lumps, don't worry—they will get strained out.

9   As soon as the curd has finished cooking, strain
it through a fine-mesh sieve. Use the back of a
spoon or a spatula to push as much through as you
can—you don't want to lose any of that great citrus
flavour! *Continued ›*

10 Gradually whisk in the butter cubes until the mixture is completely smooth and all the butter is incorporated. If the curd has cooled too much to incorporate all the butter, place it back on the double boiler for a few minutes and whisk until the butter is incorporated. You can also use an immersion blender to blend it in; this will eliminate any graininess and leave you with velvety, extra-smooth curd.

11 Cut the bottom and top off the lime. Using a sharp serrated or paring knife, starting at the top and working your way around, cut away the outside of the lime, removing as much of the white pith as possible *(Photo E, page 216)*. Holding the lime in your hand, for each segment, carefully slice the membrane to remove the fruit inside *(Photo F, page 216)*. Chop the segments into little pieces and mix into the curd. Cover and refrigerate for at least 4 hours.

TO MAKE THE YOGURT CREAM

12 Make sure the water is ice cold. Place 2 Tbsp in a small microwavable bowl, sprinkle in the gelatin, and stir to dissolve. Refrigerate until firmly set.

13 Heat the first measure of cream and the white corn syrup together over low heat to just melt the syrup. The mixture should be only warm; avoid heating it fully as it will split, giving the finished cream an unpleasant texture.

14 Heat the set gelatin in the microwave until melted (about 30 seconds) and stir it into the cream.

15 Slowly melt the white chocolate over a double boiler or on half power in a microwave. Pour the warm cream over the chocolate in three parts, mixing vigorously with a spatula between additions until smooth.

16 Place the yogurt in a large bowl. Whisk the second measure of whipping cream into the yogurt in three parts. Add the white chocolate cream mixture and the grated black lime and whisk until smooth and uniform. Refrigerate for at least 3 hours, until set *(Photo A)*.

TO ASSEMBLE THE CAKE

17 Place one of the cake halves on a cake decorating turntable or a flat serving plate. If the top domed a lot during baking, using a sharp serrated knife, trim it to flatten it out *(Photo B)*.

18 Using a stand mixer fitted with a paddle attachment, whip the yogurt cream on medium-low speed until smooth *(Photo C)*. This should only take a minute.

19 Place half of the yogurt cream in a piping bag (or a resealable freezer bag) and cut about 1 inch off the end. Pipe a generous ring of cream around the edge of the cake *(Photo D)*, leaving a bit of extra room around the edge for it to spread once the top layer is added. Fill the centre of the cake with the curd *(Photo E)*.

20 Place the other cake on top, top side down so that your cake will have a flat top, and gently press down. If your kitchen is hot or you're concerned about the frosting coming out the sides when you come to frost the top, you can transfer the cake to the freezer for 1 hour. Freezing will also help if you're planning on more intricate decorating or on covering the sides of the cake as well as the top.

21 With the cake on the turntable, spoon the remaining yogurt cream on top *(Photo F)*, spreading it out just to the edges. If desired, use an offset spatula or a knife to create a decorative pattern.

22 Grate a small amount of black lime over the top of the cake. Lightly sprinkle with fresh citrus zest and garnish with fresh edible flowers. If not serving immediately, keep it in the refrigerator, letting it sit at room temperature for about 15 minutes before serving. If your cake was quite frozen, let it defrost at room temperature for at least 1 hour before serving.

SERVING & STORAGE

Although best served the day it is assembled, this cake will keep in the refrigerator for up to three days.

TARTE TROPÉZIENNE

Serves 6 to 8—

BRIOCHE DOUGH

30 g (2 Tbsp) whole milk

13 g (1 Tbsp) fresh yeast, crumbled,
  or 8 g (2 tsp) active dry yeast

250 g (1⅔ cups) all-purpose flour

30 g (2 Tbsp) sugar

1 tsp salt

3 large eggs, at room temperature

145 g (⅔ cup) unsalted butter, cubed,
  at room temperature

CRUMB TOPPING

60 g (⅔ cup) cake flour

40 g (3 Tbsp) sugar

pinch of nutmeg

45 g (3 Tbsp) unsalted butter

Ingredients continued ›

EQUIPMENT

You will need two baking sheets and a stand
mixer fitted with a dough-hook attachment.

Although not technically a tart but a brioche, this dessert is great to finish a Sunday brunch or enjoy with a cup of tea with loved ones. Invented in the 1950s in St. Tropez, this is the first known filled brioche. The famous movie star Brigitte Bardot tasted it while filming there and loved it so much that she named it Tarte Tropézienne. Traditionally, it's filled only with pastry cream, but adding a lovely homemade compote makes it that much tastier.

It's not really possible to make brioche dough in a smaller batch size. For this recipe, the compote and pastry cream will make one Tarte Tropézienne but you will have enough brioche dough to make two bases. After baking you can freeze one base for future use, or if you want to serve the tarte tropézienne to a larger group, simply double the compote and pastry cream and fill both bases.

TO MAKE THE BRIOCHE

1   In a small bowl, warm the milk slightly so that it will activate the yeast (but not too hot or it will kill it). Add the yeast and stir *(see 'Yeast Facts,' page 39)*. Set aside for 5 minutes.

2   In a stand mixer bowl, combine the flour, sugar, and salt by hand. Make a well in the centre and add the eggs and the yeast-and-milk mixture.

3   Fit the bowl on the stand mixer and mix on low speed until all the ingredients are well combined. Stop the mixer at least once to scrape down the sides.

4   On medium-low speed, gradually add the butter, a few cubes at a time. Once all the butter has been added *(Photo A, page 198)*, turn the mixer up to medium and continue mixing for 10 to 15 minutes, until the dough is smooth and shiny and has pulled away from the sides of the bowl. *Continued ›*

5 Shape the dough into a ball and place it seam side down in the stand mixer bowl *(Photo B)*. Cover and let rise at room temperature for 1 hour, or until nearly doubled in size. If your kitchen is quite chilly, go ahead and let it rise for an extra half hour.

6 While your dough is resting, make the crumb topping. In a bowl, combine the cake flour, sugar, and nutmeg. Add the butter and, using your hands, work it into the dry ingredients until even crumbs are formed. Set aside. You can also make your pastry cream and compote at this time.

7 Once the dough has risen, punch it down. At this point it is ready to use, but it can also be wrapped in plastic wrap lightly sprayed with oil and stored in the refrigerator for up to 2 days.

8 Line 2 baking sheets with parchment paper. Divide the brioche dough into 2 balls. Lightly flour a work surface and, for each ball, either flatten it with your hands or roll it out into a 6- to 7-inch circle. Place one on each lined baking sheet and prick them all over with a fork *(Photo C)*.

9 To proof the dough, fill a pan with the hottest water you can get out of your tap (not boiling) and place it on the bottom of your oven. Place the brioche trays in the oven, close the oven door, and let the dough proof for about 1 hour, until roughly doubled in size. Do not open the oven door until the hour is up, as you want the steam to create a humid environment inside the oven.

10 Once the dough is proofed, remove the pan of water and the brioche from the oven. Preheat your oven to 385°F (195°C).

11 Using a pastry brush, brush the brioches with water. Sprinkle the crumb topping evenly over them both *(Photo D)* and bake for 12 to 15 minutes, or until the top is a golden brown. *Continued ›*

PASTRY CREAM

80 g (⅓ cup + 1 Tbsp) sugar

80 g (about 4 large) egg yolks

2 Tbsp cornstarch

¼ tsp salt

365 g (1½ cups) milk

45 g (3 Tbsp) unsalted butter, cubed

1 tsp vanilla extract or paste

RHUBARB COMPOTE

300 g (about 3 cups) rhubarb, fresh or
   frozen, cubed

100 g (½ cup) sugar

juice of ½ an orange

½ tsp vanilla extract or paste

½ tsp ground ginger

¼ tsp ground cinnamon

TO MAKE THE PASTRY CREAM

12 Place the sugar and egg yolks in a bowl and whisk until lightened in colour. Whisk in the cornstarch and salt.

13 In a saucepan over medium-low heat, heat the milk to scalding (just before boiling). Keep an eye on it as it can boil over quickly. Slowly drizzle the hot milk into the yolk mixture while continuing to whisk. If you add it too quickly, the eggs will curdle and your pastry cream will be lumpy.

14 Once all the milk has been added, transfer the mixture back to the saucepan and place over medium heat. Whisking constantly, bring the mixture to a boil and continue cooking for 1 more minute.

15 Remove from heat. If you see any lumps, immediately strain the pastry cream through a fine-mesh sieve. Add the butter and vanilla and whisk until smooth; if you want it even smoother, use an immersion blender.

16 Cover the pastry cream with plastic wrap, making sure the wrap is directly touching the surface. Refrigerate for 2 to 3 hours, until set, or up to 3 days.

TO MAKE THE RHUBARB COMPOTE

17 Combine all of the ingredients in a saucepan over medium heat. When it starts to simmer, turn the heat down to low. Continue simmering for 20 to 30 minutes, stirring frequently, until the rhubarb has broken down and become translucent.

18 Transfer the compote to a heatproof dish and set aside to cool. Store in the refrigerator until ready to use, up to 2 weeks. *Continued ›*

19 Using a serrated knife, slice one of the brioches in half horizontally. Spread the rhubarb compote over the bottom half, leaving a bit of room around the edge.

20 Loosen the cold pastry cream with a spatula and top the compote with it, again leaving a bit of room around the edge. Place the other half of the brioche firmly on top, cut side down, and gently press down. Place in the refrigerator.

21 In order for the tarte to set properly and slice cleanly, refrigerate it for at least 6 hours. It's fine to serve right after it's assembled (I often do!), but it's a bit tricky to cut without filling coming out of the sides. Slice only when ready to serve.

STORAGE

Tarte Tropézienne should be served within 48 hours of assembly. The extra baked brioche will keep for up to one day at room temperature or up to three months in the freezer.

PRALINE CHOCOLATE LOAF

Makes 2 loaves—

CAKE
290 g (2 cups) all-purpose flour
120 g (1 cup) cocoa powder
1 tsp baking powder
½ tsp salt
500 g (2½ cups) sugar
340 g (1½ cups) unsalted butter, at room
   temperature
6 large eggs
240 g (1 cup) buttermilk

CRUNCHY MILK CHOCOLATE BASE
150 g (1 cup) milk chocolate chunks
85 g (1 cup) feuilletine

CHOCOLATE HAZELNUT GLAÇAGE
50 g (⅓ cup) whole hazelnuts, peeled and
   roughly chopped
210 g (1½ cups) milk chocolate chunks
50 g (¼ cup) vegetable oil

ASSEMBLY
240 g (1 cup) Nutella
edible gold leaf, for garnish *(optional)*

INGREDIENT NOTE
Feuilletine, a crunchy praline cereal, is one of
my favourite ingredients to use in pastry. It
adds great texture to melted chocolate and a
nice light crunch to pastries. Although feuilletine is a bit difficult to substitute because of
its wafer-thin texture, cornflakes cereal makes
an acceptable option.

EQUIPMENT
You will need two loaf pans, a baking sheet, a
wire cooling rack, an instant-read thermometer, and a stand mixer fitted with a whisk
attachment.

I used to think of the loaf as only something quick and easy
to make and casual enough to eat straight out of the pan.
But as I learned from my time living in Tokyo and my
travels in France, the humble loaf can in fact be dressed up
and turned into something quite elegant. In recent years,
I've really upped my loaf game and now take great delight
in finding different ways to finish them. This loaf is definitely for the chocolate lover, and the Nutella makes it all
the more sinful.

TO MAKE THE CAKE

1   Preheat your oven to 350°F (180°C). Butter the loaf
    pans or spray them with vegetable oil.

2   Sift together the flour, cocoa powder, baking
    powder, and salt. Set aside.

3   Place the sugar and butter in a stand mixer bowl and
    mix on medium speed until the mixture is fluffy and
    has lightened considerably in colour, scraping down
    the sides of the bowl as needed. This can take up to
    5 minutes.

4   With the mixer on low speed, add the eggs two at
    a time, scraping down the sides of the bowl and
    mixing well between each addition.

5   Still on low speed, add the sifted dry ingredients in
    three parts alternating with the buttermilk in two
    parts, beginning and ending with the dry mixture.
    Scrape down the bowl between each addition.

6   Divide the batter evenly between both pans. Bake for
    55 to 60 minutes, until a toothpick comes out clean.
    If you are using dark-coloured nonstick pans, the
    loaves may bake a bit faster, so keep an eye on the
    time. As soon as the loaves are cool enough to touch,
    unmould them and place them on a cooling rack.
    Continued ›

TO MAKE THE CRUNCHY BASE

7   Line a baking sheet with parchment paper.

8   Slowly melt the chocolate over a double boiler or in a microwave on half power. Mix in the feuilletine.

9   Spread the mixture on the parchment paper in roughly a rectangular shape twice the size of one of your loaf pans, about 5 mm thick. Refrigerate it briefly, until it just starts to set. Using the base of your loaf pan as a guide, cut out two pieces of chocolate each the size of your loaf pan *(Photo A)*. Break up the crunchy base trimmings into shards and reserve them for finishing the cake later. Return both the crunchy bases and the shards to the refrigerator until you are ready to use them.

TO MAKE THE GLAÇAGE AND ASSEMBLE THE LOAF

10   Preheat your oven to 350°F (180°C).

11   Spread the hazelnuts on a baking sheet and toast for 6 to 8 minutes, until golden brown. Let cool. Once cooled, using a nut grinder or a knife, chop them into small pieces and set aside.

12   Melt the chocolate over a double boiler. Once completely melted, mix in the vegetable oil. Remove from the double boiler and let cool until the mixture reaches 40°C (104°F). Proceed to steps 13 & 14 while your glaçage cools.

13   Gently spread a few dollops of Nutella over each crunchy base. Centre one of the cakes on top of a crunchy base and place it on a wire cooling rack. Place the rack over a plate or a baking sheet to catch dripping glaçage *(Photo B)*. If your kitchen is warm, keep the second crunchy base with the shards in the refrigerator until you are ready to use them. *Continued ›*

14 Spread the remaining Nutella over the top of each loaf.

15 Once the glaçage has reached temperature, mix in the chopped hazelnuts. Using a large ladle or a measuring cup, pour the glaçage over the cake to cover the top and sides completely *(Photo C)*. If you miss any spots, use a knife or your finger to cover them.

16 Scrape the glaçage drippings off the tray back into the bowl. Position your second loaf as you did the first and cover it with the remaining glaçage.

17 Immediately top both loaves with crunchy shards, then sprinkle with edible gold leaf, if you like. Let set in the refrigerator before moving each cake to a serving plate or gift box.

STORAGE

This cake will keep covered at room temperature for up to a week. If the environment is warm, keep it in the refrigerator.

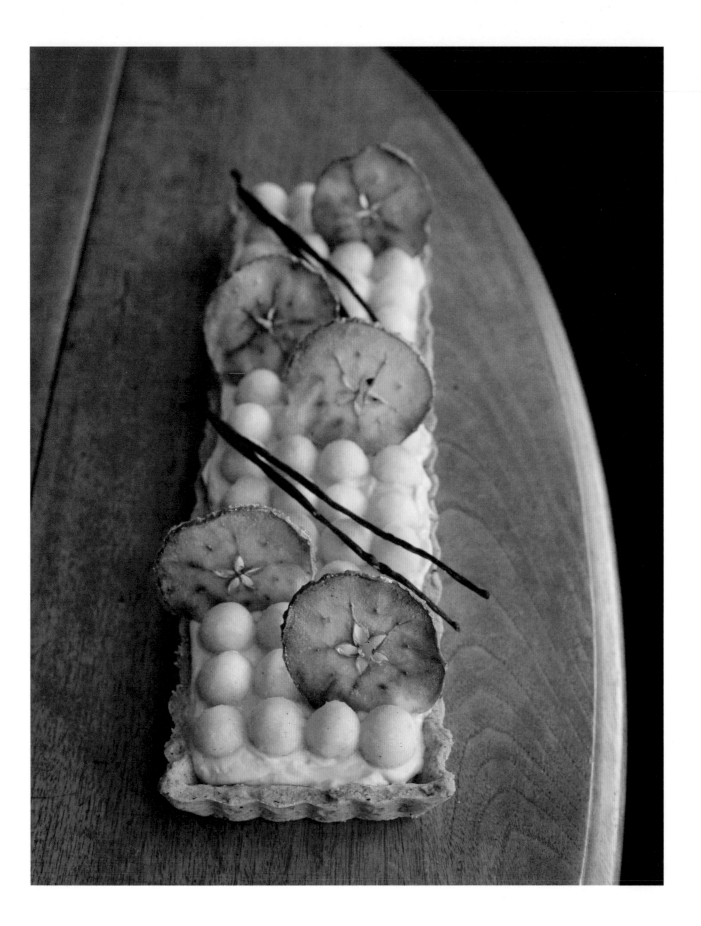

BUCKWHEAT PÂTE SUCRÉE

175 g (1 cup + 3 Tbsp) all-purpose flour

65 g (⅓ cup + 1 Tbsp) buckwheat flour

75 g (⅔ cup + 2 Tbsp) icing sugar

35 g (¼ cup) almond flour (finely ground almonds)

¼ tsp salt

145 g (⅔ cup) unsalted butter, at room temperature

1 large egg

¼ tsp vanilla extract or paste

MOLASSES WHIPPED GANACHE

100 g (¾ cup) white chocolate chunks

165 g (¾ cup) whipping cream

75 g (⅓ cup) whipping cream, cold

1 Tbsp fancy molasses (or birch syrup)

Ingredients continued page 210 ›

INGREDIENT NOTES

Buckwheat flour can be easily found in specialty organic grocery stores and in some major grocery chains. If you can't find it, simply replace it with all-purpose flour.

As birch syrup is difficult to find, this recipe calls for molasses instead, which is what I use when I make this tart at home. If you happen to have birch syrup, feel free to use it instead of molasses.

This recipe makes enough pâte sucrée for two tarts if you save the trimmings from this one. Unbaked pâte sucrée freezes very well, so you can keep the extra dough in your freezer ready to go for your next tart.

EQUIPMENT

You will need a removable-bottom tart pan (14-by-4-inch rectangular or 8-inch round), a stand mixer fitted with a paddle attachment, a baking sheet, a mandoline *(optional)*, and a melon baller.

Parisian Apple
BUCKWHEAT TART

In the fall of 2017, I, along with two teammates, had the chance to participate in a televised pastry competition in France. To get accepted to compete on the show, we had to complete a timed challenge at home during which we made a few of our own recipes.

For our entry, we wanted to show our grasp of traditional French techniques but also add a touch of Canadiana. A common way to serve potatoes in France is à la parisienne, that is, as little round balls scooped out using a tool similar to a melon baller. I've always loved the way this looks, and so my partner, Jacob, suggested we try making a tart with apples à la parisienne for our trial. We added our own local flair in the form of buckwheat flour and Jacob's favourite ingredient, birch syrup.

Our trial was on Thanksgiving weekend. Exhausted, we ended up eating this tart with our family for dessert that night. I was thrilled with the finished product, and fortunately, the judges agreed!

TO MAKE THE PÂTE SUCRÉE

1   Sift the flour, buckwheat flour, icing sugar, almond flour, and salt together in a stand mixer bowl.

2   Fit the bowl on a stand mixer fitted with a paddle attachment. Add the butter and mix on low speed for 1 to 2 minutes, until the mixture looks sandy *(Photo A, page 208)*.

3   Add the egg and vanilla and continue to mix on low speed for another minute or two, stopping when the dough is barely mixed *(Photo B, page 208)*. Some of the dry ingredients may still be visible. Be sure not to overmix or the dough will become tough and hard to work with. Turn the dough onto the counter and press it down by hand to work in the last of the dry ingredients.

4   Shape the dough into one large rectangle, or a circle if you are using a round tart pan. Wrap well in plastic wrap and let rest in the refrigerator for 3 hours, or up to 4 days. You can also freeze it for up to 3 months. *Continued ›*

5　Slowly melt the chocolate over a double boiler or on half power in a microwave. In a saucepan, heat the first measure of whipping cream until scalding (just before boiling).

6　Pour the hot cream over the chocolate in three parts, mixing vigorously with a spatula between additions until smooth. Slowly whisk in the second measure of cream (cold) and the molasses. The mixture will be liquid.

7　Let the ganache set in the refrigerator for at least 4 hours or overnight. It will thicken slightly but still be a bit liquid.

TO ROLL OUT THE PÂTE SUCRÉE AND BAKE THE TART SHELL

8　Prepare your tart pan by greasing the inside with a small amount of butter, making sure no bits of butter remain visible in the pan.

9　Remove the pâte sucrée from the refrigerator and lightly flour a work surface and both sides of the dough. The dough may need a few minutes at room temperature before you can work with it.

10　Roll out the dough into a roughly rectangular shape 3 to 4 mm thick *(Photo C)*, or round if you are using a round tart pan, checking it often to ensure it's not sticking to your work surface. It helps to give the dough a quarter turn after each roll, flip it over frequently, and flour as needed. As the dough gets thinner it becomes more delicate and difficult to flip over; just keep gently rotating it and lightly flouring as you roll.

11　Pick up the dough rectangle and centre it over the tart pan. If your dough has gotten quite warm or you've taken a long time to roll it out, it might be difficult to lift without tearing it. Don't worry—you can piece it back together once in the pan. *Continued ›*

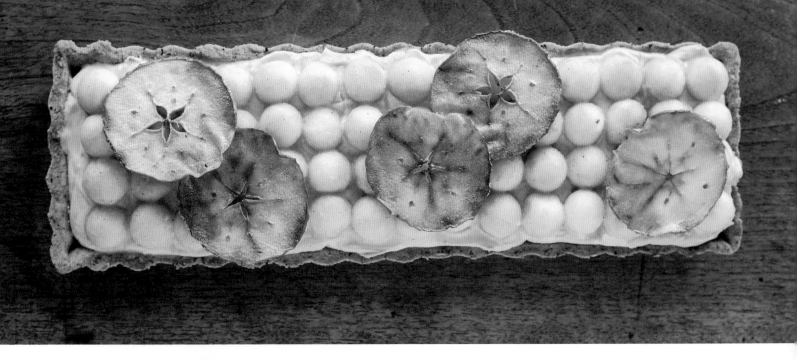

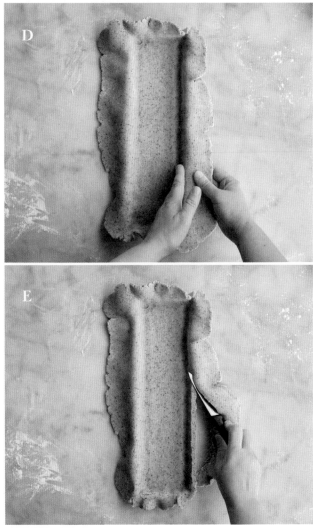

12 Work the dough into the pan using your fingers to lift the edge of the dough and your thumbs to gently press it down *(Photo D)*. Work around all the edges until the dough is pressed flat in the pan to cover the bottom as well as the sides and into the corners, patching any tears as you go.

13 Run a sharp knife along the top rim of the pan to trim off excess dough *(Photo E)*. If you save the trimmings you will have just enough pâte sucrée for another tart if you roll it efficiently and piece bits together by hand. It will keep in the refrigerator for 3 days or in the freezer for 3 months.

14 Using a fork, lightly poke holes in the bottom of the shell to prevent air bubbles from forming while baking. Refrigerate for at least 15 minutes. While the shell is chilling, preheat your oven to 375°F (190°C).

15 Bake the chilled shell for 18 to 20 minutes, until the edges and bottom are a light golden brown. If at any point during baking the pastry puffs up in one area, poke it with a sharp knife to let steam escape. Cool completely before assembling the tart. *Continued ›*

APPLE CHIPS
1 Granny Smith apple
sugar, for dipping

APPLES À LA PARISIENNE
2 Tbsp lemon juice
5 Granny Smith apples
50 g (¼ cup) sugar
2 Tbsp unsalted butter
1 tsp vanilla extract or paste
whole vanilla beans, for decoration
 (optional)

TO MAKE THE APPLE CHIPS

16 Preheat your oven to 250°F (120°C) and line a baking sheet with parchment paper. Slice an apple into thin slices using a mandoline. If you don't have a mandoline, use a sharp knife to slice as thinly as possible. Choose the slices from the middle of the apple with the star-shaped centres. Remove any seeds that have not naturally fallen out.

17 Dip each slice lightly in sugar on both sides and spread out on the parchment paper *(Photo F)*. Bake for 50 minutes to 1 hour, until golden brown. As soon as the apples come out of the oven, using a fork or tongs, remove them from the parchment and place them on a cooling rack to harden, being careful as they will be very hot. They will stick to the parchment paper if allowed to cool for too long. Set aside.

TO PREPARE THE APPLES À LA PARISIENNE

18 Place the lemon juice in a bowl. Peel one of the apples and, using a mini melon baller, scoop out individual balls *(Photo G)*. Try to space out your scoops so they all come out as round as possible. As you add them to the bowl, toss them in the lemon juice so they don't brown. Repeat with the remaining apples.

19 Melt the sugar and butter together in a small saucepan. Add the apple balls and sauté for about 2 minutes. The aim is not to cook them but rather to poach them in the syrup. Remove from heat and stir in the vanilla. Cool completely before assembling the tart. *Continued* ›

20 Carefully remove the sides of the tart pan, leaving the shell positioned on the bottom of the pan.

21 Using a stand mixer fitted with a paddle attachment, on medium-low speed, whip up the molasses ganache until soft peaks form. Keep a close eye on it: if it overwhips it will start to separate and end up grainy.

22 Fill the tart shell with the whipped ganache. Gently spread it around *(Photo H)*, being careful not to break the shell.

23 Once the apples à la parisienne have cooled completely, spoon them out of the liquid and arrange them over the ganache, either in a pattern *(Photo I)* or randomly. If not serving immediately, refrigerate the tart until ready to serve. Top with the apple chips just before serving (they will go soft if refrigerated). Garnish with whole vanilla beans.

Note: Once filled and topped with the apples, the tart will be quite heavy. Leave it on the removable tart base to serve it rather than trying to transfer it to another plate.

SERVING & STORAGE

This tart is best served on the day it's assembled. It will keep in the refrigerator for up to two days, but keep in mind that the tart shell will go very soft.

Grapefruit Lavender
PAVLOVAS

Serves 6—

MERINGUE
120 g (about 4 large) egg whites
1 tsp white wine vinegar
pinch of salt
150 g (¾ cup) sugar
½ tsp vanilla extract or paste
2 tsp cornstarch

Ingredients continued ›

EQUIPMENT
You will need a baking sheet, a stand mixer
fitted with a whisk attachment, a paddle
attachment, and a piping bag fitted with a star
tip (for individual nests). A culinary torch is
handy for the brûlée, but your oven broiler
will also work great.

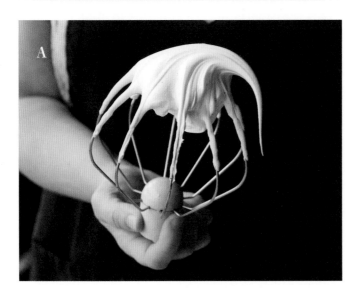

*I've always loved making meringue and get great satis-
faction in seeing egg whites and sugar whip up into a
silky, shiny cloud. In this version I make elegant little
individual filled nests, which are always a hit. For a
simpler, more casual option, you can make Eton Mess
instead (see page 217).*

*After baking, the meringue really needs to sit in the
oven for at least three hours—and maybe quite a bit more,
if it's humid—to properly dry out. That's why I consider
this pavlova great for an event that I know I have coming
up: I can prepare all of the parts up to four days in
advance and quickly put it together right before serving.*

TO MAKE THE MERINGUE

1   Make a piping template for the individual meringue
    nests by tracing six 3-inch circles on a piece of
    parchment paper. Flip the template over so the
    lines are face down on your baking sheet. If you're
    making Eton Mess, simply line a baking sheet with
    parchment paper.

2   Preheat your oven to 250°F (120°C). Set up your
    piping bag so it's ready to be filled.

3   Place the egg whites in a stand mixer bowl fitted
    with a whisk attachment and whip on medium-low
    speed. As soon they start to foam, add the vinegar
    and salt. Continue to whip until very soft peaks form.

4   Still on medium-low speed, add the sugar 2 table-
    spoons at a time, mixing about 2 minutes between
    each addition. This process will take over 10 minutes.
    Once all the sugar is in, turn the mixer up to medium-
    high and whip until stiff, glossy peaks form *(Photo A)*.
    Be careful not to whip it too far or it will lose some
    of its shine and start to split.

5   Turn the mixer off and add the vanilla and corn-
    starch. Mix on low speed until just combined.
    Continued ›

GRAPEFRUIT CURD

zest of 3 grapefruits

225 g (1 cup + 2 Tbsp) sugar

2 large eggs

3 large egg yolks

180 g (¾ cup) grapefruit juice, freshly squeezed (1–2 large)

225 g (1 cup) unsalted butter, at room temperature, cubed

LAVENDER WHIPPED GANACHE

270 g (1¼ cups) whipping cream

1 Tbsp dried culinary lavender

160 g (1¼ cups) white chocolate chunks

110 g (½ cup) whipping cream, cold

ASSEMBLY

2 grapefruits

sugar

dried lavender, for garnish

INGREDIENT NOTES

You'll roughly need four or five grapefruits to make the curd and have enough for finishing. Squeezing fresh grapefruits will give your curd a much brighter flavour than buying grapefruit juice in a carton. When you're zesting the grapefruit, only zest the outside of the skin and not the bitter white pith.

Try to find dried culinary lavender that is brightly coloured and has a strong aroma.

The curd and whipped ganache will need to chill for at least four hours before assembly.

6 At this stage, it's important to work quickly. Glue down the four corners of your parchment paper with a bit of meringue *(Photo B)*. To pipe the nests, fill a piping bag fitted with a star tip with the meringue. Starting in the centre of a traced circle, pipe a thin layer of meringue to fill the circle *(Photo C, bottom right)*. Pipe two rings of meringue along the edge of the circle, working your way up to make a nest *(Photo D)*. Repeat with the remaining circles.

If you're making Eton Mess, using a spoon, simply drop dollops of meringue on the parchment paper.

7 Bake for 45 minutes. Do not open the oven door during baking. When done, turn off the oven and leave the meringue inside for several hours. The nests should become firm as they cool and dry out completely. Meringue really doesn't like humidity, so if you do a lot of cooking or you live in a humid climate, leave it in your turned-off oven for up to 2 days. After it's dried out, store it in a well-sealed container. If your oven runs a bit on the hot side, the meringue might have turned out beige in colour—perfectly fine.

TO MAKE THE GRAPEFRUIT CURD

8 In a bowl, rub the grapefruit zest into the sugar using your fingers to bring out the oils. Add the eggs and egg yolks and whisk until well combined. Add the grapefruit juice and whisk again.

9 Transfer to a double boiler. Cook over low heat for 25 minutes. The mixture will lose about half of its volume. It's important to whisk frequently to avoid the eggs scrambling and leaving you with a curd that has an unpleasant texture. If you do see some lumps, don't worry—they will get strained out. *Continued ›*

10 As soon as the grapefruit mixture has finished cooking, strain it through a fine-mesh sieve. Use the back of a spoon or a spatula to push as much cream through as you can—you don't want to lose any of that great grapefruit flavour!

11 Gradually whisk in the butter cubes until the mixture is completely smooth and all the butter is incorporated. If the curd has cooled too much, place it back on the double boiler for a few minutes and whisk until the butter is incorporated. You can also use an immersion blender to blend it in; this will eliminate any graininess and leave you with velvety, extra-smooth curd. Cover and refrigerate at least 4 hours.

TO MAKE THE WHIPPED GANACHE

12 In a saucepan, heat the first measure of whipping cream until scalding (just before boiling). Turn off the heat, stir in the lavender, and cover tightly. Steep for 10 minutes. While the lavender is steeping, slowly melt the chocolate over a double boiler or on half power in a microwave.

13 Strain out the lavender through a fine-mesh sieve, using the back of a wooden spoon or a spatula to push the lavender against the sieve to extract maximum flavour. Pour the hot lavender cream over the chocolate in three parts, mixing vigorously with a spatula between additions until smooth. Slowly whisk in the second measure of cream (cold). The mixture will be liquid.

14 Let the ganache set in the refrigerator for at least 4 hours or overnight. It will thicken slightly but still be a bit liquid. *Continued ›*

TO ASSEMBLE THE PAVLOVAS

15 Do the assembly just before serving. Cut the bottom and top off the grapefruits. Using a sharp serrated or paring knife, starting at the top and working your way around, cut away the outside of the grapefruits, removing as much of the white pith as possible *(Photo E)*. Holding each grapefruit in your hand, for each segment, carefully slice the membrane to remove the fruit inside *(Photo F)*. Cut each segment into 3 or 4 pieces. Pat the pieces with a paper towel to soak up excess juice.

16 Place the grapefruit pieces on an unlined baking sheet. Sprinkle the top of each with sugar. Using a culinary torch, torch each piece until the sugar is melted and slightly charred *(Photo G)*. If you don't have a torch, set the broiler on your oven to high and place the tray as close to the broiler as possible. Remove as soon as the sugar starts to bubble. Set aside.

17 Using a stand mixer fitted with a paddle attach-ment, whip up the ganache until soft peaks form. Keep a close eye on it: if it overwhips it will start to separate and end up grainy. Fit a piping bag with the same piping tip you used to pipe the nests and fill it with whipped ganache. Remove the grapefruit curd from the refrigerator.

18 Fill the bottom of each nest with curd. Pipe whipped ganache in a ring along the top edge of each nest, going around about twice *(Photo H)*. Place 4 or 5 grapefruit segments in the centre of each nest and top with a sprinkling of lavender. Serve immediately.

SERVING & STORAGE

Pavlova is best eaten soon after it's put together. The parts on their own do keep well. The lavender whipped ganache and grapefruit curd can be kept in the refrig-erator for up to five days. Baked meringue will keep at room temperature for up to a week as long as the environment is dry.

Eton Mess—

Not confident in your piping skills? Your meringue nests didn't quite end up in the shape you wanted? No worries—you can always serve Eton Mess! Eaten traditionally at Eton College in England during cricket matches, Eton Mess is basically bits of broken meringue with fruit and cream served in individual dessert cups. It takes all the stress out of finishing a perfect dessert, and you can modernize it a bit by serving it in Mason jars or glass jars. If you're not a fan of grapefruit and lavender, simply top the meringue with fresh fruit and whipped cream instead.

Sunday Funday
BIRTHDAY CONES

On my son's fourth birthday, I sent him to school with chouquettes (cream puffs) thinking he would be thrilled. It was very convenient for me because I could easily grab the things I needed from the Bake Shop and minimize fuss. When I picked him up that day, I asked him if his class liked the desserts I sent. He replied in a sad voice: "They were okay, but I was really hoping for cupcakes with sprinkles on them like the other kids get." Deep down I knew that I had put no effort into making his treats and hadn't really listened to what he wanted. That upcoming Sunday he would be having a little party with friends and I decided that I would make his cake dreams come true.

I remembered that when I was little, some of the kids would have birthday ice cream cones with cake baked into the bottom. What if I made those? And instead of topping them with overly sweet buttercream, I could make two whipped ganaches, a vanilla and a chocolate, and swirl them together on top to look like soft-serve ice cream. Benoît would love it!

For an authentic flashback to my childhood, I went out and bought cake mix. Well, despite reading blog posts and checking out photos, my cones came out of the oven a complete disaster. I hadn't mixed the cake batter enough, and they all exploded and overflowed. I was mortified (the owner of Duchess Bake Shop can't make a cake from a mix)!

I needed a solution. I remembered that for every birthday and special occasion, my mother-in-law makes her famous one-bowl Miracle Whip chocolate cake. It's super moist and flavourful and always turns out. She suggested I try her recipe and fill the base of the cones only half full. Well, they worked out beautifully, and Benoît's face lit up when I presented them to him. Even though these are so different from the things I usually bake, that day, I was so proud of my creation.

VANILLA WHIPPED GANACHE

160 g (1¼ cups) white chocolate chunks
270 g (1¼ cups) whipping cream
110 g (½ cup) whipping cream, cold
2 tsp vanilla extract or paste

MILK CHOCOLATE WHIPPED GANACHE

145 g (1 cup) milk chocolate chunks
270 g (1¼ cups) whipping cream
110 g (½ cup) whipping cream, cold

CAKE CONES

24 flat-bottomed ice cream cones
290 g (2 cups) all-purpose flour
200 g (1 cup) sugar
30 g (¼ cup) cocoa powder
1½ tsp baking soda
1½ tsp baking powder
235 g (1 cup) Miracle Whip
240 g (1 cup) water
2 tsp vanilla extract or paste
sprinkles, for garnish

INGREDIENT NOTES

My mother-in-law insists that you must use Miracle Whip—no other mayonnaise will do. I also found that you need to use the old-school ice cream cones (with flat bottoms). I experimented with gluten-free cones but found the texture quite unpleasant after baking, so I suggest avoiding those.

The whipped ganaches need to chill for at least four hours before whipping up. You can prepare the ganaches up to three days in advance, but the cones are best eaten the day they are baked and finished.

EQUIPMENT

You will need a stand mixer fitted with a whisk attachment, two muffin pans, three large piping bags, and a star-shaped piping tip.

TO MAKE THE WHIPPED GANACHES

Do the following separately for each ganache:

1   Slowly melt the chocolate over a double boiler or on half power in a microwave. In a saucepan, heat the first measure of whipping cream until scalding (just before boiling).

2   Pour the hot cream over the chocolate in three parts, mixing vigorously with a spatula between each addition until smooth.

3   Slowly whisk in the second measure of cream (cold) and the vanilla (for the vanilla version only). The mixture will be liquid.

4   Let the ganache set in the refrigerator at least 4 hours or overnight. It will thicken slightly but still be a bit liquid.

TO MAKE THE CAKE CONES

5   Preheat your oven to 350°F (180°C). Place the cones in the muffin pans, 1 per cavity.

6   Sift together the flour, sugar, cocoa powder, baking soda, and baking powder. Add the Miracle Whip, water, and vanilla and mix for 2 minutes in a stand mixer or using a hand mixer.

7   Using an ice cream scoop or a spoon, carefully fill each cone halfway with batter. Be careful not to overfill or the cake will overflow in the oven.

8   With a steady hand, place the muffin pans in the oven. Bake for 23 to 25 minutes, until a toothpick comes out clean *(Photo A)*.

9   As soon as the cones are cool enough to handle, using a toothpick, poke a few holes in the bottom of each. This will release steam and prevent the cake inside from getting soggy. Place on a wire rack to cool. *Continued ›*

TO FINISH THE CONES

10 Separately for each ganache, using a stand mixer fitted with a paddle attachment, whip until soft peaks form. Keep a close eye on it: if it overwhips it will start to separate and end up grainy.

11 Have ready a piping bag fitted with a star tip *(Photo B, left)*. Place each ganache in its own piping bag with no piping tip. Using scissors, cut the tips off the ganache bags (about 2 cm) *(Photo B, centre & right)*. Insert both ganache bags into the piping bag fitted with the star tip *(Photo C)*.

12 Pipe a large swirl of ganache onto the top of each cone *(Photo D)*. Top with sprinkles.

SERVING & STORAGE

If, like me, you don't have a cupcake carrier, you can make one out of cardboard. Simply use the base of a cone as a guide to trace and cut out circles. Cover with wrapping paper and poke holes where the cones will go *(see photo, page 219)*.

The cones are best eaten the day they are baked. They are good at room temperature for up to three hours and can be refrigerated for up to five hours (after that, they will go soggy).

CROQUEMBOUCHE

If there was ever a recipe that should be read from one end to the other before starting, it's this one!

A cream puff (chouquette) tower covered in spun sugar is the stuff dreams are made of. In France, a croquembouche (translated to 'crunch in the mouth'), often with a nougatine base, is traditionally served on special occasions such as weddings, baptisms, and birthdays. It's the perfect celebratory dessert because everyone gets to share in the fun of breaking cream puffs off the tower and eating them together.

I've had many home bakers tell me that making a croquembouche once in their life is on their baking bucket list, and that's why I wanted to include a recipe in this book. Even for a professional pastry chef, making a croquembouche can be quite a challenge, and working with burning-hot sugar tends to make everyone a bit nervous. Despite this, it's definitely possible to make one at home, and can even be a ton of fun! I think that it's wonderful to challenge yourself in the kitchen and to keep learning by making things that might take you a bit out of your comfort zone. I still get nervous and excited every time I make one!

Remember that although the pastry cream and chouquettes can be made days in advance, they should only be filled and dipped in the caramel on the day you plan on serving the croquembouche.

The Golden Rules—

- Build the croquembouche on the plate or dish on which you plan on serving it. Trying to transfer a croquembouche after it's been built is very risky and may result in tears.
- After your chouquettes are filled, it will take 45 minutes to an hour to build your croquembouche. Make sure to set aside some time so you can give it your undivided attention and assemble it from start to finish with no distractions. If that means turning off your phone and sending your kids to play outside, then do it.
- Do not refrigerate the croquembouche or bring it into a hot and humid environment. Humidity (including in the refrigerator) will melt the sugar, which is the glue holding everything together, and eventually the tower may end up falling over. For example, attempting to serve a croquembouche at a wedding held in a greenhouse (which has been done) is a recipe for disaster a few hours into the reception.
- Don't drive with it for several hours, and make sure someone is always holding it if it's being transported in the car. Croquembouches simply don't travel well, and trying to drive one to a faraway location is risky.
- A croquembouche should be served no more than six hours after assembly. The best time to eat it is two or three hours after it's been made. The chouquettes will progressively soften, the pastry cream inside will get warm, and eventually it will no longer be possible to 'snap' individual chouquettes off the structure.
- If the croquembouche breaks or a large chunk falls off, it is possible to reassemble it if most of your chouquettes are still intact. If you have leftover caramel, you can heat it back up and use it to carefully glue the structure back together. Another option is to use a torch to heat the caramel on the chouquettes, allowing you to stick them back together.

My friend Dayna with her first croquembouche.

Different ways to assemble a croquembouche—

PILE IT UP

The easiest way is to simply pile up the chouquettes that have been dipped in caramel. Purists would say that this is not a traditional croquembouche, which is almost always hollow in the middle. And making it hollow is really the main challenge and most of the fun!

USE A MOULD

For something larger than about 50 chouquettes, like the croquembouches we used to make at Duchess Bake Shop, you can purchase a professional croquembouche mould, a large hollow metal cone. One of these can set you back upwards of a couple hundred dollars. The cone is flipped over and the tower built on the inside, starting at the bottom. After reaching the top, the cone gets flipped right side up and the tower pops out.

USE A STYROFOAM CONE

Styrofoam cones are available at floral supply stores and some craft stores. The cone is lined with parchment paper and then chouquettes are built up against it around the outside, from the bottom up. The cone is then removed from the bottom. The main problem with this scenario is that the croquembouche is a very delicate structure, and trying to lift it up and pull out the cone not only is anxiety-inducing for almost anyone, it can easily result in disaster. The cone can always be left inside the croquembouche and served that way, but the beauty of the tower being hollow is lost.

BUILD IT FREESTYLE (MY PREFERRED WAY!)

At home I build my croquembouche by making a freestanding tower, generally not going higher than 40 or 50 chouquettes. I like to use a little paper cone *(see template, page 231)* as a guide to build around so my structure isn't too lopsided. I've seen daring bakers build freestanding structures 80 or 90 chouquettes high, but their engineering skills are far better than mine.

Working with caramel—

- Caramel is extremely hot. Use the utmost caution when working with it. Even a little bit on your skin or the ends of your fingers will burn you.
- Although it is tempting to use plastic gloves when dipping the chouquettes in the hot caramel, I highly advise against it. You can get a much better grip with your bare fingers *(Photo A)*, and if you get any caramel on the plastic glove, it will burn onto your hand (ouch!). Metal tongs will work for a while, but after a few dips, you'll get hard chunks of caramel sticking to them, making them difficult to use.
- If you drop a chouquette in the hot caramel as you're trying to dip it, do not attempt to fish it out with your hands. Instead, consider it lost and use a spoon to remove it onto a piece of parchment or a silicone mat *(Photo B)*.
- It's important to only cook your caramel to a light amber colour because it will continue to darken after you've removed it from the heat.
- If the caramel starts to harden, put it back on the heat for 30 to 60 seconds, just until it melts again.
- To finish, the croquembouche is wrapped in spun sugar. At Duchess Bake Shop we do this using a special tool with lots of little metal prongs sticking out of it. The best recreation of this tool at home is to cut the ends off a wire whisk using wire cutters *(Photo C)*. If you don't want to ruin a whisk, just use two forks back-to-back.

Now that we've talked about all the scary stuff, it's time to have fun!

CHOUQUETTES

1 double batch Pâte à Choux *(page 66),*
    just made
1 large egg yolk, beaten

PASTRY CREAM

140 g (⅔ cup + 2 Tbsp) sugar
140 g (about 7 large) egg yolks
40 g (¼ cup) cornstarch
¼ tsp salt
640 g (2⅔ cups) whole milk
60 g (¼ cup + 1 Tbsp) unsalted butter,
    cubed, at room temperature
120 g (⅔ cup) milk chocolate, melted
½ tsp vanilla extract or paste

CARAMEL

600 g (3 cups) sugar
180 g (¾ cup) water
180 g (½ cup + 1 Tbsp) white corn syrup
    or glucose

INGREDIENT NOTE

For the chocolate, I like to use Valrhona Caramélia milk chocolate, but you can use any milk or dark chocolate you like.

EQUIPMENT

You will need a stand mixer fitted with a paddle attachment, three baking sheets, a piping bag fitted with a small round tip (#803 or #804), and a second piping bag.

I recommend serving the croquembouche on a flat serving plate. If you want to serve it on a stand, you may need to find yourself a sturdy stool to stand on so you are working at the right height.

TO PIPE AND BAKE THE PÂTE À CHOUX

1. Before making your dough, make templates by cutting 3 pieces of parchment paper to the size of your baking sheets and, on each, drawing 15 circles 1½ inches wide (about the size of a shot glass), about 2 inches apart. Flip the templates over so the lines are face down on the baking sheets.

2. Preheat your oven to 375°F (190°C).

3. As soon as your pâte à choux is made, use a small amount to glue down the corners of the templates to the baking sheets. This will prevent the templates from slipping around while you're piping your chouquettes.

4. Fill a piping bag fitted with a small round tip (#803 or #804) with the pâte à choux.

5. Position your piping tip a few centimetres above the template over the centre of a circle. Pipe out dough until it reaches the edge of the circle, repeating for all circles on both trays. If you have any extra dough, pipe extra chouquettes where you can fit them on the tray. Use your finger to gently run egg yolk over the top of each chouquette, smoothing down any bumps as you go *(Photo D)*.

6. Immediately bake the chouquettes for 30 minutes. Do not open the oven door during baking. After 30 minutes, open the oven door for 5 to 10 seconds to let the built-up steam escape and slightly dry out the dough. Bake for about another 5 to 8 minutes, until you can feel that the outside of the dough has crisped up. They should be a dark golden brown in colour.

7. Once baked, the chouquettes keep at room temperature, covered, for 2 days. If you didn't fill them right away and the choux has gone soft, re-crisp them in the oven for 4 to 6 minutes at 350°F (180°C) before filling them. The baked chouquettes can also be frozen for up to 2 months; in that case, place them frozen in a 350°F (180°C) oven until warmed through and crispy (6 to 8 minutes). *Continued ›*

D

E

F

TO MAKE THE PASTRY CREAM

8 Place the sugar and egg yolks in a bowl and whisk until lightened in colour. Whisk in the cornstarch and salt.

9 In a saucepan over medium-low heat, heat the milk to scalding (just before boiling). Keep an eye on it as it can boil over quickly. Slowly drizzle the hot milk into the yolk mixture while continuing to whisk. If you add it too quickly the eggs will curdle and your pastry cream will be lumpy.

10 Once all the milk has been added, transfer the mixture back to the saucepan and place over medium heat. Whisking constantly, bring to a boil and continue cooking for 1 to 2 more minutes.

11 Remove from heat. If you see any lumps, immediately strain the pastry cream through a fine-mesh sieve. Add the butter, melted chocolate, and vanilla, and whisk until smooth; or if you want it even smoother, use an immersion blender.

12 Cover the pastry cream with plastic wrap, making sure the wrap is directly touching the surface. Refrigerate for 2 to 3 hours, until set and cold, or up to 3 days.

TO ASSEMBLE THE CROQUEMBOUCHE

13 Line a baking sheet with a piece of parchment paper and make a cone template *(Photo E; template on page 231).*

14 Sort through the chouquettes and pick out the ones that are the roundest and easiest to hold *(Photo F).* You will need about 40 or 45 chouquettes filled, but the more you have to work with, the easier it will be. Turn the chouquettes over so that the flat sides are facing up. Using the tip of a paring knife, poke a small hole in the bottom of each. *Continued ›*

15 Loosen the cold pastry cream with a spatula to make it easier to pipe. Fill a piping bag with the pastry cream and cut a small hole off the end of the bag. For each chouquette, insert the tip of the piping bag into the hole and fill *(Photo G)*. Wipe away any excess pastry cream coming out of the hole. Set the chouquettes aside.

16 To make the caramel, place the sugar, water, and corn syrup in a saucepan. Cook on medium-low heat until a light amber in colour. Remove from heat and immediately proceed to the next step. Even off the heat, the sugar will continue to cook and darken as it sits, so it's important to work quickly.

   Note: If your caramel becomes very dark, almost black and smells burnt, don't panic, just clean your pot *(see step 25, page 230)*, and get a new batch of caramel cooking.

17 Make sure your baking sheet is lined with a clean piece of parchment paper. Once the bubbles in the caramel have died down, you can start dipping your chouquettes.

18 Pick up each chouquette by its sides and dip it top down into the caramel *(Photo H)*. Let the excess caramel drip off and place it caramel side down onto the lined baking sheet *(Photo I)*. It will harden into a nice flat circle of shiny caramel *(Photo J)*.

   Warning! Be very careful when working with the caramel in this way. If it touches your skin it will burn you instantly. If you drop a chouquette in the caramel, do not attempt to retrieve it with your hands. Scoop it out with a spoon and set it on the parchment paper to dry.

19 Once all of your chouquettes are dipped and cooling top down on the baking sheet, place your cone template in the centre of the dish on which you will be serving the croquembouche. Lift a chouquette from the parchment paper and place it on the plate, disk facing up, near the outer edge of the cone but not touching it. *Continued ›*

20 Take the next chouquette, dip the side of it in the caramel *(Photo K)* and stick it to the chouquette on the plate. Work your way around the cone *(Photo L)*, dipping and glueing each chouquette to make a ring (you should have 7 to 9 chouquettes as your ring base). Using a spoon, drizzle caramel where the chouquettes are touching to ensure that they are well stuck together *(Photo M)*.

Note: Try not to stick any caramel to the paper cone. It's meant only as a guide to keep your tower round and will be difficult to remove later if it's covered in caramel.

21 For the second layer, dip the side of a chouquette in caramel to stick it to the row below, disk facing out *(Photo N)*. You may need to hold each chouquette in place to dry a bit before glueing the next one. Build each level a bit closer to the centre as you work your way up the cone. Make sure you use enough caramel to really stick each chouquette together and drizzle caramel in the cracks after each level *(Photo O, page 230)*. Remember that the caramel is your glue, and without enough glue, you won't have a stable structure.

22 Once you've reached level 3 or 4, remove your paper cone *(Photo P, page 230)*. Take a pair of scissors, gently cut it all the way to the bottom, and pull it out. If the paper has stuck to the chouquettes, pull at it gently until you get it out.

23 Continue to work your way inwards, dipping and glueing the chouquettes until you've closed up the top *(Photo Q, page 230)*. If at any point your caramel becomes too set to dip, place it back on the heat until it just starts to melt and take it off again. *Continued ›*

24 As soon as you've completed the tower, take your altered whisk (or two forks held back to back) and dip it in the caramel. The caramel should be starting to set and thicken. Pull sugar strings around the cone to make decorative tendrils *(Photo R)*. The sugar cools as you stretch it out, so you can use your hands to pull it into long strands. Do as little or as much as you'd like. If you plan on adding decorative or edible flowers, do so only right before serving.

25 To clean up, fill your caramel saucepan with water and put it back on the stove. If you got caramel on any utensils, add them to the saucepan. The boiling water will melt away all the sugar, which you can then pour down the sink.

SERVING & STORAGE

Serve the croquembouche within six hours of assembly. There's really no way to eat it other than with your hands. It always takes one brave person to crack the top one, and everyone will quickly follow suit.

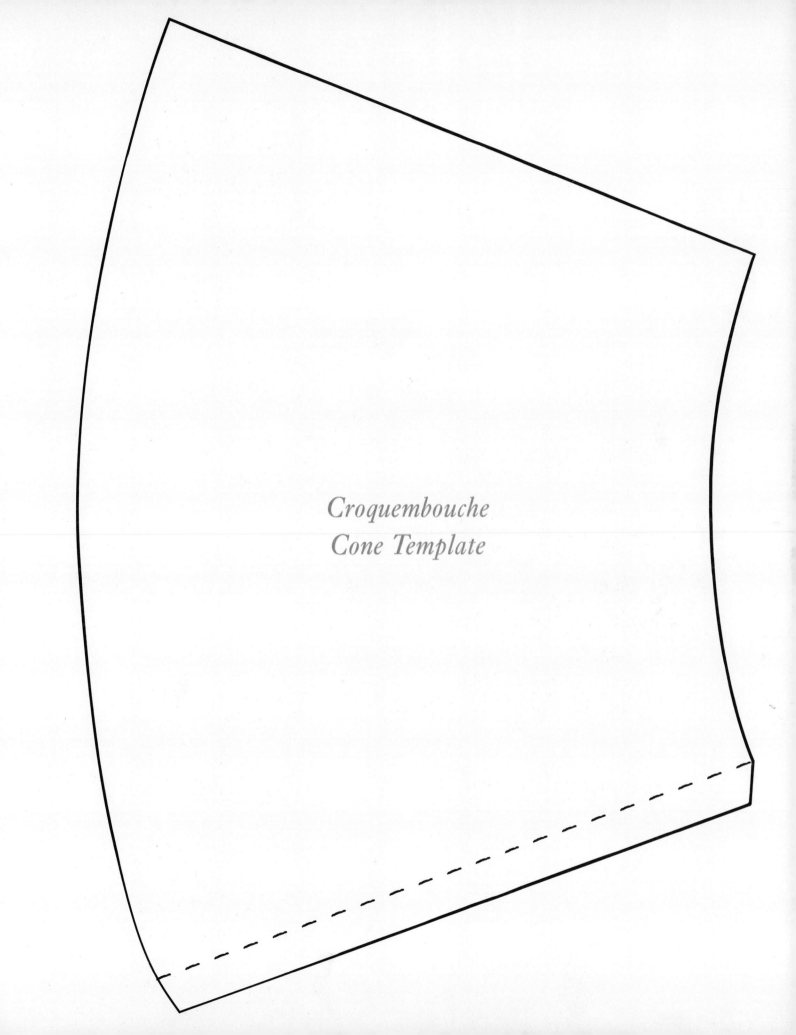

Croquembouche
Cone Template

Dans mon jardin
IN MY GARDEN

MY DAILY LIFE is usually very stressful and exhausting, and I often find myself with little or no time to myself. The most therapeutic relief for me is the simple quiet moments I get to spend in my garden in the evenings after the kids have gone to bed. All of my daily stresses and worries seem to melt away and I somehow go to bed feeling a little lighter in mind, body, and spirit.

Every February, I sit down and plan my summer garden, tweaking and fixing based on what I learned the previous summer. Someone once told me to plant the things that you like to eat, which is a mantra that I stick to. For me that includes planning my garden around the crops I will be pickling and canning. I live in a well-established neighbourhood, so there's also an abundance of fruit trees and berry bushes in my yard or in a neighbour's, which drives the jams and preserves that I make each year.

Canning and making jam is something I find extremely relaxing. Mixing the fruit with sugar, getting the brine ready, and snacking on berries or beans are all part of my canning ritual. I also like to have a friend over to spend the afternoon with me making pickles or jam, moments that I dearly cherish.

"HOW LOVELY IS THE SILENCE OF GROWING THINGS."
—EVAN DICKEN

Backyard
RHUBARB CRISP

Serves 8—

CRUMB TOPPING
145 g (1 cup) all-purpose flour
175 g (1 cup firmly packed) golden brown sugar
55 g (½ cup) old-fashioned rolled oats
115 g (½ cup) unsalted butter, melted and cooled

FILLING
500 g (4 cups) chopped rhubarb, fresh or frozen, in 1-inch pieces
150 g (¾ cup) sugar
40 g (¼ cup) all-purpose flour
½ tsp ground cinnamon
vanilla ice cream, to serve

EQUIPMENT
You will need an 8-by-8-inch or 9-by-7-inch baking dish.

In Alberta, rhubarb grows in abundance, and even if you don't grow it yourself, your neighbour is bound to have some extra to give you. This super-simple rhubarb crisp is perfect for a casual patio meal or barbecue on a summer's evening.

This dessert freezes really well unbaked, as I learned growing up from my mother, who would make several to freeze for the winter months. To avoid tying up a baking dish, you can use a disposable aluminum pan. Seal it in a plastic bag along with a bit of paper with the temperature and baking time written on it for a little reminder. Take it out in January and bake it from frozen for a little taste of summer.

PROCEDURE

1 Butter the baking dish. Preheat your oven to 375°F (190°C).

2 To make the crumb topping, in a bowl, combine the flour, brown sugar, and oats. Add the butter and, using your hands, work it into the dry ingredients until large clumps form. Set aside.

3 In a separate bowl, place all the filling ingredients and toss to combine.

4 Spread out the filling in the bottom of the baking dish. Sprinkle the crumb topping evenly overtop.

5 Bake for 35 to 40 minutes, until bubbling around the sides and the rhubarb in the centre is soft. Check it after 15 or 20 minutes, and if the top is already looking quite brown, cover it with foil. If baking from frozen, you may need to add 5 to 10 minutes to the baking time.

SERVING & STORAGE
Rhubarb crisp is best eaten warm out of the oven with a scoop of vanilla ice cream. It will keep at room temperature for up to two days. Warm leftovers for 30 seconds in the microwave before serving.

APPLE CORNMEAL
Upside-Down Cake

Serves 8 to 10—

APPLES

4 or 5 apples
115 g (½ cup) unsalted butter
175 g (1 cup firmly packed) golden brown sugar
½ tsp ground cinnamon
¼ tsp ground ginger
¼ tsp ground nutmeg
pinch of ground cloves

BATTER

180 g (1¼ cups) all-purpose flour
55 g (⅓ cup) cornmeal or polenta (finely ground cornmeal)
½ tsp baking soda
½ tsp salt
115 g (½ cup) unsalted butter, at room temperature
100 g (½ cup) sugar
2 large eggs
1 tsp vanilla extract or paste
180 g (¾ cup) buttermilk
cream or ice cream to serve *(optional)*

INGREDIENT NOTE

If you don't have the luxury of having an apple tree in your yard, I recommend buying Granny Smith or Honeycrisp apples for this recipe.

EQUIPMENT

You will need a 9-inch cast-iron pan or a 9-inch cake pan.

A few years ago, Jacob lovingly built us a wood-fired oven in our yard. He finished it in late summer just as the apples were starting to fall from our tree. This cake is the first thing I baked in that oven, and it came out so beautifully that it has become our dessert of choice whenever we light up the oven and have people over.

This cake is also wonderful baked in a cast-iron pan in a regular oven. With the cast iron you can cook your apples on the stove and then transfer the pan directly into the oven for baking. You can also use a regular frying pan to cook the apples and then bake the cake in a cake pan.

PROCEDURE

1 If you're using a cake pan, butter it. Preheat your oven to 350°F (180°C).

2 Peel and core the apples and cut them into quarters or, if really large, into eighths *(see tips, page 133).*

3 To prepare the apples, in a cast-iron pan over medium heat, melt the butter. Add the brown sugar, spices, and apples and stir to coat. If you don't have quite enough apples to fill up the pan, cut up another apple and add it. Cook for about 5 minutes, stirring occasionally. The apples should still be a bit firm. Remove from heat and set aside.

4 To make the batter, whisk together the flour, cornmeal, baking soda, and salt, and set aside.

5 Place the butter and the sugar in a stand mixer bowl. Cream on medium speed for 2 minutes, scraping down the sides as needed.

6 Add the eggs one at a time, mixing well after each addition. Add the vanilla. *Continued ›*

7 With the mixer on low speed, gradually incorporate the buttermilk, stopping the mixer a few times to scrape down the sides of the bowl. At this stage the mixture will look lumpy and slightly separated. Once all the buttermilk has been mixed in, add the dry ingredients. Mix on low until well combined.

8 If you're using a cake pan, transfer the apples and sauce to the pan. Pour the batter over the apples.

9 Bake for 35 to 40 minutes, until a toothpick inserted in the centre comes out clean.

10 Let the cake cool for about 10 minutes before inverting it onto a plate or serving platter large enough to catch all the syrup. If any of the apples have stuck to the bottom of the pan, place them back on top of the cake.

SERVING & STORAGE

This cake is best served warm out of the oven with ice cream or a drizzle of heavy cream. It will keep, covered at room temperature, for up to two days. When having it as a leftover, warm it up for 30 seconds in the microwave before serving.

Summer Fruit
CLAFOUTIS

Serves 6 to 8—

FOR AN 8- OR 9-INCH DISH

300 g (2–2½ cups) pieces of mixed fruit
70 g (⅓ cup) sugar
zest of 1 small lemon
75 g (½ cup) all-purpose flour
pinch of salt
2 large eggs
190 g (¾ cup) whole milk
icing sugar, to serve

FOR A 10- OR 11-INCH DISH

400 g (4–4½ cups) mixed fruit
100 g (½ cup) sugar
zest of 1 large lemon
100 g (⅔ cup) all-purpose flour
pinch of salt
3 large eggs
310 g (1¼ cups) whole milk
icing sugar, to serve

INGREDIENT NOTES

If you are using cherries for your clafoutis and have only a few cups to pit, if you don't have a cherry pitter you can use the end of a straw to push the pits out.

EQUIPMENT

You can use any ceramic or glass baking dish. I've included ingredient measurements for two different round dish sizes, but either way, there's a bit of flexibility.

Clafoutis is a quick and easy baked summer custard dessert. It's the perfect platform for showcasing all kinds of fresh summer fruit: raspberries from the garden, plums from the market, Saskatoon berries from the freezer. I like to mix a berry with a stone fruit, with one of them a bit more on the tart side (pictured: raspberry/plum and Saskatoon berry/ Rainier cherry).

PROCEDURE

1 Butter the baking dish or spray it with vegetable oil. Preheat your oven to 375°F (190°C).

2 Combine the fruit, half the sugar, and the lemon zest in a bowl. Set aside.

3 In a bowl, whisk together the flour, remaining sugar, and salt. Set aside.

4 In a separate bowl, whisk the eggs for about 1 minute, until thickened and foamy. Add the dry ingredients and whisk until there are no more lumps. Drizzle in the milk and mix until well combined.

5 Spread the fruit evenly over the bottom of the dish. Slowly pour the batter overtop.

6 Bake for 35 to 40 minutes, until lightly browned around the edges and well set in the middle. Cool completely.

7 Once cool, keep refrigerated until serving. Dust lightly with icing sugar to serve.

SERVING & STORAGE

Clafoutis is traditionally served cold, though it can be served warm. It can be made in advance and will keep refrigerated for up to two days.

Beet & Potato
PANCAKES

Makes 8 to 10 pancakes—

INGREDIENTS

250 g beets, peeled and grated (about 2 cups loosely packed)

500 g yellow-flesh potatoes, peeled and grated (about 4 cups loosely packed)

2 Tbsp all-purpose flour

1 tsp caraway seeds

1 tsp salt

½ tsp ground black pepper

2 large eggs

vegetable oil, for frying

smoked salmon, sour cream, and sprigs of fresh dill, to serve *(optional)*

Our sister restaurant, Café Linnea, makes a wonderful Scandinavian-inspired savoury vegetable pancake with two things I have lots of in my garden: potatoes and beets. I make my own version of these at home and enjoy them with different toppings—such as Linnea's choice combination of smoked salmon, sour cream, and fresh dill—sometimes for both lunch and dinner on the same day!

PROCEDURE

1   Place the grated beets and potatoes in a large bowl.

2   Mix together the flour, caraway seeds, salt, and black pepper. Sprinkle over the potatoes and beets. Toss to coat.

3   Whisk the eggs, add them to the potatoes and beets, and combine. The batter will be on the wet side.

4   Coat the bottom of a frying pan with vegetable oil. Be generous with the oil as you will be shallow-frying the pancakes. Turn the heat on medium.

5   When the oil starts to shimmer, scoop about ½ cup of the batter into the pan. Flatten well with the back of a spatula. Cook for 3 to 4 minutes, gently shaking the pan every so often to prevent the pancake from sticking.

6   When the bottom is nice and crispy, gently flip over. Continue to cook for another 2 or 3 minutes, until slightly browned and crispy.

7   Transfer the pancake onto a piece of paper towel to soak up excess oil. Keep warm in the oven while you continue to cook the remaining pancakes, adding more oil to the pan as needed.

STORAGE & SERVING

These pancakes will keep for up to five days in the refrigerator. Reheat them gently in the microwave or in a frying pan before serving.

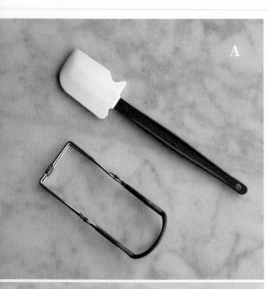

A Note on
CANNING & JAM MAKING

The fruits of a bountiful garden just beg to be canned, pickled, or made into jam so that they can be enjoyed year round. If you've never tried these arts, I hope some of the recipes in this chapter will inspire you to give them a shot.

To develop your skills, there are entire books devoted to canning methods, sanitation guidelines, food acidity, and scientific explanations. Some of my favourites are Preservation Society Home Preserves *and* Blue Ribbon Preserves. *Here I cover some basics to get you started.*

THINGS TO KEEP IN MIND

- Try to use fruits and vegetables that are as fresh as possible.
- Follow recipes exactly, especially when pickling. Canning can be a bit tricky because you're dealing with varying acidities in foods, and if the science of this is not properly taken into account, it can lead to dangerous food poisoning. All of the pickle recipes that I use have been given to me and I have made them many times, so I know they are safe.
- There's a bit more leeway when it comes to fruit jams because of the amount of sugar and the natural acidity in fruit, but erring on the side of caution is always best.
- It's best to weigh your ingredients rather than measure them. Canning is a precise science, and precision is the key to safety and success.
- Use a wooden spoon or a heatproof spatula *(Photo A, top)* for stirring foods that will be canned. Some metal spoons (such as iron, copper, or steel) can react with high-acidity foods to cause discoloration or form toxic compounds.
- When filling the jars, if you get any drips, brine, or jam on the lids or seals, gently wipe them away with a damp paper towel to make sure that the rim is completely clean before sealing.
- After the jars have been processed in the water-bath canner or pot, always check that they have sealed properly. For Bernardin-style jars, the little button in the middle of the lid should be down. For Weck jars, you should not be able to pull the lid off—it should be well stuck down.

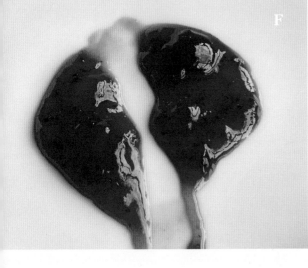

JARS & SANITIZING

There are several different kinds of canning jars available on the market today. The two most popular types are offered by Bernardin, with a screw cap and snap lid closures *(Photo B)*, and Weck, with rubber rings, glass lids, and clips *(Photo C)*. Both are great for canning.

Whichever you settle on, make sure that your lids, seals, and rubber rings are brand new every time you use them. It's very important to make sure your lids and seals are clean and to properly sanitize your jars before you begin canning to kill any bacteria present. To do so, heat your oven to 250°F (125°C) and put your jars in for 20 minutes.

You will need a water-bath canner *(Photo D)* or a very large pot with a lid to properly process your pickles and jam. Water-bath canners usually come with a handy insert for holding the jars; if you are using a large pot, you will need to place something on the bottom to protect the jars, like a metal rack *(Photo E)* or a dish towel.

Before you start your jamming or pickling, fill the canner ¾ full with water, bring to a rolling boil, and then turn the heat off. Once your jars are ready for processing, place them in the hot water using a jar lifter *(Photo A, bottom)* and bring it back to a rolling boil. Then start your timer and process for the time indicated in your recipe.

THE WRINKLE TEST

The best option for checking whether your jam is set is the 'wrinkle test': Put two small plates in the freezer. Once the jam has been bubbling for 5 minutes, start to look for signs that it's nearly done. The jam will start to look shiny and the fruit almost translucent; also, when dripping off a spoon or spatula, the droplets will want to stick together rather than run off like water. When you see either of these signs, remove from heat, remove a cold plate from the freezer, and place a small dollop of jam on the plate. Refrigerate it for 2 minutes, and then push back on the jam with your finger. If it wrinkles and doesn't flow back into itself right away *(Photo F)*, the jam is set. If it needs more time, turn the heat back on, keeping an eye on it and checking it again within a few minutes of it coming back to a boil.

Rhubarb Cherry Kirsch
JAM

Makes four or five 250-ml jars

INGREDIENTS

750 g (about 7 cups) rhubarb, fresh or frozen, cut into ½-inch pieces

750 g (3¾ cups) sugar

100 g (½ cup) freshly squeezed lemon juice

530 g (about 3½ cups) pitted sour cherries, fresh or frozen

50 g (¼ cup) kirsch liqueur

EQUIPMENT

You will need a fine-mesh sieve, a water-bath canner or a very large pot with a lid, and four or five 250-ml canning jars with the appropriate seals.

A cherry pitter is useful, but if you don't have one, you can use the end of a straw to push the pits out.

'More rhubarb?!' By the beginning of August, I'm always looking for new ideas to deal with the crazy amount of rhubarb I have to use up. One of my dear friends has an Evans sour cherry tree, and she kindly shares her bounty with me every year. I discovered that these cherries go really well with rhubarb. This jam is the perfect way to showcase all the delicious fruit that grows in our yards.

PROCEDURE

1 Sanitize your jars for 20 minutes in a 250°F (125°C) oven *(see 'Jars & Sanitizing,' page 245)*.

2 Combine the rhubarb, sugar, and lemon juice in a saucepan or a copper pot. Bring to a simmer over medium-low heat, stirring frequently with a heat-proof spatula or a wooden spoon.

3 Once the rhubarb has softened and the sugar has completely dissolved, use a slotted spoon to remove the rhubarb pieces, leaving as much liquid in the saucepan as possible. Reserve the cooked rhubarb in a bowl.

4 Add the cherries to the saucepan and bring to a boil. Cook until they have softened and shrivelled up *(Photo A, page 248)*. Remove from heat.

5 Place a fine-mesh sieve over the bowl of cooked rhubarb. Pour in the cherries and liquid and, using the back of a spoon or spatula, press them over the rhubarb, extracting as much liquid as possible *(Photo B, page 248)*. Discard the cherry pulp.

6 Transfer the cherry juice and rhubarb back into the saucepan *(Photo C, page 248)*. Bring to a boil. *Continued ›*

7 Continue to cook over medium-low, stirring gently, until the jam has thickened and the rhubarb has broken down *(Photo D)*. It should remain at a rolling boil while cooking. The jam is ready when it begins to cling to a wooden spoon or a heatproof spatula, falling off in clumps, and has passed the 'wrinkle test' *(see 'The Wrinkle Test,' page 245)*. This should take between 15 and 25 minutes.

8 When the jam is set, immediately remove from heat and stir in the kirsch. Using a ladle or a glass measuring cup, pour into the canning jars to within ¼ inch of the rim, seal well, and process in a water-bath canner for 5 minutes. If you live at an altitude of over 3,000 feet, add 5 minutes to the processing time.

9 Carefully remove the jars from the water bath and leave to cool undisturbed overnight. The next day check to make sure that the jars have sealed properly.

STORAGE

Unopened jars will keep in a cool, dry place for up to a year. Store opened jars in the refrigerator for up to three months.

Apricot Raspberry
JAM

Makes five or six 250-ml jars ——

INGREDIENTS
**1 kg apricots, weighed after pitting and
 quartering
900 g (4½ cups) sugar
60 g (¼ cup + 1 Tbsp) freshly squeezed
 lemon juice
1 vanilla bean, sliced lengthwise,
 or 1 Tbsp vanilla paste
500 g raspberries, preferably fresh**

INGREDIENT NOTE
Take advantage of the summer market season
to get your hands on delicious in-season apricots. Buy a few extra to make sure you end up
with a full kilogram after they've been pitted.

    Macerating the apricots—adding sugar to
enhance the flavour and draw out liquid—is
key to the success of this jam.

EQUIPMENT
You will need a water-bath canner or a very
large pot with a lid, and five or six 250-ml
canning jars with the appropriate seals.

*My good friend Sarah and I are both 'jam people.' We spend
a lot of time not only eating jam but also talking about the
different jams we're experimenting with in our kitchens.
We both agree that apricots aren't that appealing for eating
fresh, but as far as stone fruit goes, they are the best for
making delicious jam. Sarah got creative one day and
tossed some raspberries into her traditional apricot jam,
and voilà! Our new favourite jam was born.*

PROCEDURE
1   Mix the apricots, sugar, lemon juice, and vanilla
 bean or paste together in a non-reactive bowl
 (ceramic, plastic, or glass). Cover well with plastic
 wrap and set aside to macerate for at least 1 hour or
 overnight.

2   The next day, sanitize your jars for 20 minutes in
 a 250°F (125°C) oven *(see 'Jars & Sanitizing,'
 page 245).*

3   Place the macerated fruit in a saucepan or copper
 pot. If you used a vanilla bean, remove it at this
 point. Bring to a boil over medium-low heat, stirring
 gently and frequently with a heatproof spatula or a
 wooden spoon. Cook until the apricots are quite soft
 and are starting to break down.

4   Gently stir in the raspberries and continue to cook
 at a rolling boil, stirring occasionally, being extra
 cautious to minimize breaking up the raspberries.
 Cook until the jam begins to cling to a wooden
 spoon or a heatproof spatula, falling off in clumps,
 and has passed the 'wrinkle test' *(see 'The Wrinkle
 Test,' page 245).* This should take 10 to 15 minutes.
 Continued ›

5   When the jam is set, immediately remove from heat. Using a ladle or a glass measuring cup, pour into the canning jars to within ¼ inch of the rim, seal well, and process in a water-bath canner for 5 minutes. If you live at an altitude of over 3,000 feet, add 5 minutes to the processing time.

6   Carefully remove the jars from the water bath and leave to cool undisturbed overnight. The next day check to make sure that the jars have sealed properly.

STORAGE

Unopened jars will keep in a cool, dry place for up to a year. Store opened jars in the refrigerator for up to three months.

Savoury
CRABAPPLE JELLY

Makes five or six 250-ml jars —

INGREDIENTS
1.75 kg crabapples
1.25 L (5 cups) water
800 g (4 cups) sugar
170 g (½ cup) honey
55 g (¼ cup) apple cider vinegar
1 sprig fresh sage

INGREDIENT NOTE
The colour of your jelly all depends on what kind of crabapples you use. It can range from a light pink to a dark red.

EQUIPMENT
You will need a water-bath canner or a very large pot with a lid, and five or six 250-ml canning jars with the appropriate seals. You will also need a jelly bag, a nut milk bag, or a large piece of cheesecloth.

My friend Camilla Wynne, the brilliant author of my favourite book on preserves, Preservation Society Home Preserves, *was kind enough to pass on this great recipe. With a yearly abundance of crabapples available to me, this is a really useful recipe to have in my repertoire. This jelly is extremely good served with cheese or biscuits or for glazing poultry.*

Camilla uses apple cider vinegar and sage to create this savoury version. Another acid could easily be substituted, such as sherry vinegar, wine vinegar, or verjus, as could another fresh herb, like rosemary, thyme, or even dried chilies. This recipe can also be turned into a sweeter jelly by omitting the vinegar altogether.

PROCEDURE

1   Halve the crabapples (or quarter them if large). Remove the stems and blossom ends and discard. Place them in a large pot and add the water. Bring to a boil over high heat.

2   Once boiling, reduce the heat to medium-low and simmer for about a half hour, until the crabapples have softened and broken down.

3   If you're using a jelly bag or a nut milk bag, wet the bag and suspend it over a deep receptacle. Pour the mixture into it and allow it to drip overnight at room temperature.

   If you're using cheesecloth, line a large sieve with it and suspend the sieve over a deep bowl. Pour in the crabapple mixture and allow it to drip overnight at room temperature. To keep the juice free from solids and ensure a perfectly crystalline jelly, never squeeze the bag or force the pulp through.

4   The next day, sanitize your jars for 20 minutes in a 250°F (125°C) oven *(see 'Jars & Sanitizing,' page 245). Continued ›*

5 Transfer the collected crabapple juice to a wide, heavy-bottomed pot and add the remaining ingredients. Bring to a boil over medium heat.

6 Cook at a rolling boil, stirring frequently and skimming off any excess foam, until the jelly begins to cling to a wooden spoon or a heatproof spatula, falling off in clumps, and has passed the 'wrinkle test' *(see 'The Wrinkle Test,' page 245)*. This should take 20 to 30 minutes. Once the setting point has been reached, turn off the heat, remove and discard the sage sprig, and skim off any excess foam.

7 Using a ladle or a glass measuring cup, fill the canning jars to within ¼ inch of the rim, seal well, and process in a water-bath canner for 5 minutes. If you live at an altitude of over 3,000 feet, add 5 minutes to the processing time.

8 Carefully remove the jars from the water bath and leave to cool undisturbed overnight. The next day check to make sure that the jars have sealed properly.

STORAGE

Unopened jars will keep in a cool, dry place for at least a year. Store opened jars in the refrigerator for up to three months.

Crabapple Rhubarb
SYRUP

My family likes to use this syrup to make spritzers by mixing it with sparkling water, ginger ale (kid friendly!), or white wine. This syrup also goes really well with brandy and is lovely in cocktails or poured over ice cream.

Makes 1 to 1½ litres—

INGREDIENTS

1 kg crabapples, weighed after trimming
1 kg rhubarb, cut into 1-inch pieces
750 g (3 cups) water
40 g (3 Tbsp) fresh lemon juice, strained
300–500 g sugar

INGREDIENT NOTES

The colour of your syrup all depends on what kind of crabapples and rhubarb you use. The colour can range from a light pink to a dark purple-red.

EQUIPMENT

You will need a large piece of cheesecloth, and a glass bottle or jar.

PROCEDURE

1 Wash and dry the bottle or jar you will be using to store the syrup.

2 Halve the crabapples (or quarter them if large) and remove the stems and blossom ends. Weigh the trimmed crabapples to make sure you have 1 kg.

3 In a saucepan over medium heat, combine the crabapples, rhubarb, and water. Gently bring to a boil, and then turn the heat down and simmer for 20 to 30 minutes, until the fruit is soft. Occasionally stir and mash it with a large wooden spoon to help it break down and release its juices.

4 Line a large sieve or strainer with a piece of cheesecloth and suspend it over a deep bowl. Pour in the cooked fruit and leave to drip overnight at room temperature. To avoid your syrup ending up cloudy, do not squeeze the fruit but rather let the juice drip out on its own.

5 The next day, weigh the juice you've collected and pour it into a saucepan over medium heat, along with the lemon juice. Add the sugar—you will need half the weight of the juice collected. For example, if you collected 700 g of juice, add 350 g of sugar.

6 Bring to a boil over medium-low heat. Boil for 5 minutes, stirring frequently and skimming off any excess foam. Pour into clean, dry bottles or jars.

SERVING & STORAGE

To make a simple drink, mix 1 part syrup with 3 parts sparkling water, ginger ale, or white wine. The syrup will keep, refrigerated, for up to three weeks.

Makes three 1-litre jars—

INGREDIENTS

3 garlic cloves, peeled
3 bay leaves
1½ tsp mustard seeds
6–9 fresh dill flowers
15–21 pickled hot banana pepper rings,
  or dried hot peppers of your choice
pickling cucumbers, scrubbed and dried,
  ends trimmed *(see 'How to Keep Your*
  Pickles Crisp,' page 260)
1 Tbsp pickling spices
960 g (4 cups) water
960 g (4 cups) pickling vinegar
135 g (½ cup) pickling salt
200 g (1 cup) sugar

INGREDIENT NOTES

Pickling spices are a pre-made spice blend, commonly found in most grocery stores.

If you can't find pickling salt, kosher salt is a good replacement. Pickling vinegar is typically 5% acidity white distilled vinegar.

Pickles come in all shapes and sizes, so knowing exactly how many you need to fill a jar can be tricky. It takes quite a few pickles to tightly pack a jar. A good way to guess is to trial-pack them prior to making your brine.

Not everyone likes banana peppers, and some may cringe at the thought of using the jarred ones for their pickles. Heat can be added through a variety of different kinds of dried hot peppers, but it's a bit of a gamble in terms of how many to add. Jacob, my partner, prefers these pickles made with Thai bird's-eye chilies; when using those I only add two or three to each jar.

EQUIPMENT

You will need a piece of cheesecloth or a tea infuser ball, a water-bath canner or a very large pot with a lid, and three 1-litre jars.

Hilary's Sweet & Spicy
PICKLES

I still remember the first time my friend Hilary cracked open a jar of these for me. They were sweet, sour, and spicy all at once, and I couldn't get enough of them. She was kind enough to share this family recipe with me, and I've been making it for years now. When I plant my garden in the spring, I set aside space for pickling-cucumber plants to make sure I have plenty to pickle for the winter.

Feel free to use any size jars. I use one-litre jars, and they pack a lot of cucumbers. If you run out of brine, you can quickly boil more and dip back into the same packet of pickling spices. I like to reserve a jar for lengthwise slices of cucumber to use for hamburgers and sandwiches.

PROCEDURE

1 Sanitize your jars for 20 minutes in a 250°F (125°C) oven *(see 'Jars & Sanitizing,' page 245)*.

2 In each sterilized jar, place 1 garlic clove, 1 bay leaf, ½ tsp mustard seeds, 2 or 3 fresh dill flowers, and 5 to 7 banana pepper rings.

3 Tightly pack cucumbers into each jar, leaving as little wiggle room as possible.

4 Wrap the pickling spices in cheesecloth secured with kitchen twine (or use a tea-infuser ball). Make brine by placing the water, pickling vinegar, pickling salt, sugar, and pickling spices in a saucepan and bringing to a boil. Let boil for 5 minutes.

5 Remove from heat, remove the pickling spices, and immediately pour the hot brine over the cucumbers to within about ½ inch of the top. Remove any air bubbles with a plastic spatula or a plastic knife. Discard any unused brine. *Continued ›*

HOW TO KEEP YOUR PICKLES CRISP

Ensuring that cucumbers stay crisp once pickled is a priority for many people. The ideal scenario is to pickle cucumbers that are freshly picked from the garden with little or no yellow on them. If you start with a soft cucumber, it will remain that way—there is no way to crisp it up for pickling.

Start by cutting off any discoloured ends as well as the blossom ends on the cucumbers (if you're not sure which was the blossom end, trim both ends) and making sure that they are well scrubbed and clean. Prepare an ice bath and immerse your cucumbers in it for at least two hours before pickling. If you can't pickle the day you pick your cucumbers, keep them in ice-cold water in your refrigerator for up to two days.

Another common way to ensure that your pickles stay crisp is to add a bit of 'pickle crisp' (pure calcium chloride), which can easily be found in any store that carries canning supplies. I've never found the need to use it, but many people swear by it.

6   Seal the jars, making sure to wipe any rims and lids that may have gotten brine on them with a damp paper towel. Process in a water-bath canner for 15 minutes. If you live at an altitude of over 3,000 feet, add 5 minutes to the processing time.

7   Carefully remove the jars from the water bath and leave to cool undisturbed overnight. The next day, check to make sure the jars have sealed properly.

STORAGE

The flavour of these pickles develops with time and is best if they are left alone for at least six weeks before serving. Unopened jars will keep in a cool, dry place for up to a year. Store opened jars in the refrigerator for up to three months.

Old-Fashioned Pickled
DILL BEANS

Makes two 1-litre jars—

INGREDIENTS
**500–750 g (1–1.5 lb) yellow beans,
  cleaned and trimmed**
8 fresh dill flowers
725 g (3 cups) water, for brine
240 g (1 cup) white vinegar
65 g (¼ cup) pickling salt

INGREDIENT NOTES
It takes quite a few beans to tightly pack a jar.
A good way to guess how many jars you'll
need is to trial-pack them prior to blanching
the beans. Plan for a some extra beans because
they will shrink a bit with blanching.

   Make sure that your beans are still firm and
that they haven't started to fade too much in
colour or turn white. Remember that if you
start with a soft bean, it will remain that way—
there is no way to crisp it up for pickling *(see
note, facing page)*.

EQUIPMENT
You will need a water-bath canner or a very
large pot with a lid, and two 1-litre Mason
jars with the appropriate seals.

*This is a treasured family recipe passed down from my
grandmother Courteau, who was an avid gardener. She
would make these in large quantities, up to a dozen jars at
a time, in accordance with the bounty of her garden. She
would painstakingly sort through her beans, picking ones
that were long, straight, and just the right colour to pickle.
Several members of our family have carried on the tradition of making these every year. At every family function,
you can bet that a jar of these salted beans will be opened
and devoured by young and old alike.*

PROCEDURE
1   Sanitize your jars for 20 minutes in a 250°F (125°C)
    oven *(see 'Jars & Sanitizing,' page 245)*.

2   Fill a large bowl with cold water and ice cubes. Set
    aside.

3   Bring a large saucepan of water to a boil. Add the
    yellow beans and boil for 3 minutes if small and
    tender, or 4 minutes if large and thick.

4   Drain the beans and immediately plunge them into
    the ice water to stop the cooking process. Let stand
    for 4 minutes. Drain and set aside.

5   Put 2 dill flowers into the bottom of each sterilized
    jar. Pack beans into the jars snugly to within 1 inch
    of the top, trimming the longer ones down as needed
    so that they will fit. Pack 2 more dill flowers into
    each jar.

6   Make brine by combining the water, vinegar, and
    pickling salt in a saucepan over medium heat. Bring
    to a simmer and immediately remove from heat.
    Continued ›

7   Pour the hot brine over the beans to within ½ inch of the top. Remove any air bubbles with a plastic spatula or a plastic knife.

8   Seal the jars, making sure to wipe off any rims and lids that may have gotten brine on them with a damp paper towel. Process in a water-bath canner for 15 minutes. If you live at an altitude of over 3,000 feet, add 5 minutes to the processing time.

9   Carefully remove the jars from the water bath and leave to cool undisturbed overnight. The next day check to make sure the jars have sealed properly.

STORAGE

The flavour of these beans develops with time and is best if they are left alone for at least six weeks before serving. Unopened jars will keep in a cool, dry place for up to a year. Store opened jars in the refrigerator for up to three months.

FRUIT KETCHUP
Ketchup aux fruits

I was introduced to ketchup aux fruits in my late twenties as a classic accompaniment to tourtière (French-Canadian meat pie, see page 105). Before that I had always had my tourtière with store-bought ketchup, and I was an instant convert: now I wouldn't dream of serving tourtière—or any other meat dish—without it!

This recipe makes quite a lot of ketchup. I freeze mine in two-cup portions and take it out as needed.

PROCEDURE

1 If using fresh tomatoes, using a paring knife, score the bottom of each tomato with an X. Fill a large bowl with ice and water and set aside.

2 Bring a large pot of water to a boil and drop in the tomatoes. Boil for about 1 minute, until the scored peel starts to curl away. Immediately transfer to the ice water to stop them from cooking. Peel the skin off the tomatoes using the back of a paring knife or a butter knife. Dice the tomatoes.

3 Place the pickling spices in cheesecloth secured with kitchen twine or in a tea-infuser ball.

4 Place all the ingredients in a large saucepan. Bring to a boil, and then turn the heat down to a simmer. Simmer on low heat for about 1½ hours, until the fruit and tomatoes have broken down.

5 Let the ketchup cool down before portioning into jars or resealable plastic bags.

STORAGE

Ketchup aux fruits will keep in the refrigerator for three weeks or in the freezer for six months.

Makes about 7 cups (about 1½ litres)—

INGREDIENTS

12 ripe medium tomatoes, or 2 × 796 ml cans diced tomatoes, drained

1 tsp pickling spices

5 apples (Jonagold or Golden Delicious), peeled, cored, and diced *(see tips, page 133)*

3 medium onions, diced

½ red bell pepper, seeded and diced

½ green bell pepper, seeded and diced

450 g (2¼ cups) sugar

180 g (¾ cup) white vinegar

85 g (¼ cup + 2 Tbsp) cider vinegar

2 Tbsp tomato paste

2 tsp salt

INGREDIENT NOTES

For the fruit, you can substitute the apples with peaches or pears—or do a mix of all three.

EQUIPMENT

You will need cheesecloth or a tea-infuser ball.

Acknowledgements—

This book is the culmination of several years of hard work and would not have been possible without the support of so many amazing people. I would like to thank my parents, Sylvia and André, and my parents-in-law, Cindy and Leo, for helping us at home and being so generous with their time. To Dayna and François for feeding us and being the most amazing friends as well as to Sarah A., the best friend anyone could ask for. Thank you to the very best editor (and sister!), Mona-Lynn Courteau, for keeping me on my toes and on track. To all of the friends and family who helped with recipe testing, I am truly thankful. Thank you to Garner Beggs and to all of the staff who kept the Bake Shop running smoothly and allowed me the time to write this book. Finally I would like to thank Sarah Hervieux, the most amazing, creative, talented person I know. Your eye for detail, beauty, and design is inspiring. This book would not exist without you, and I am thankful that I've gotten to work with you on this project.

(Above, from left to right) Rose, Giselle, Jacob, and Benoît.

(Left) Sarah, our designer and photographer.

INDEX